Income Equity Among U.S. Workers

Richard T. Curtin

The Praeger Special Studies program, through a selective worldwide distribution network, makes available to the academic, government, and business communities significant and timely research in U.S. and international economic, social, and political issues.

Income Equity Among U.S. Workers

The Bases and Consequences of Deprivation

PRAEGER SPECIAL STUDIES IN U.S. ECONOMIC, SOCIAL, AND POLITICAL ISSUES

Praeger Publishers New York London

Library of Congress Cataloging in Publication Data

Curtin, Richard T
Income equity among U.S. workers.

(Praeger special studies in U.S. economic, social, and political issues)
Bibliography: p.
Includes index.
1. Wages—United States. 2. Income distribution—United States. 3. Labor and laboring classes—United States—1970- I. Title.
HD4975.C87 1977 301.5'1 76-24349
ISBN 0-275-23780-X

PRAEGER SPECIAL STUDIES
200 Park Avenue, New York, N.Y., 10017, U.S.A.

Published in the United States of America in 1977
by Praeger Publishers,
A Division of Holt, Rinehart and Winston, CBS, Inc.

789 038 987654321

Printed in the United States of America

ACKNOWLEDGMENTS

The late Professor Warren L. Smith was the first to spark my interest in the study of income distribution equity, both because income equity is an important goal of public policy in its own right, and because its attainment is important for reasons of economic stability. Between the spark of initial interest and the completion of this book, Burkhard Strumpel contributed generously to every facet of its development. His insights into the behavior of mass publics improved both the underlying theoretical structure and its empirical implementation.

This book is an outgrowth of a larger research project concerned with the development of a system of social indicators of economic well-being. Supported through National Science Foundation grants GS-3244 and GS-36832, this research was performed at the Survey Research Center of The University of Michigan. The original sets of survey data and complete documentation can be obtained from the Social Science Archive (No. 3512), Institute for Social Research, P. O. Box 1248, Ann Arbor, Michigan 48106.

F. Thomas Juster, James N. Morgan, Harold T. Shapiro, and Ephraim Yuchtman Yaar offered insightful criticism and advice, especially in the preliminary stages of this study. Throughout the analysis, Laura Klem and Robert Snider gave generously of their time and skills. Anne Lloyd provided invaluable editorial assistance, and Sue Hudson prepared the manuscript with expert care.

The completion of the research would have been impossible without the skills and cooperation of very many people. The samples used in the study were drawn under the supervision of Irene Hess; the interviewing was directed by John Scott, and the coding by Joan Scheffler. The data were managed and compiled through the use of the OSIRIS computer-software system developed by the Institute for Social Research, under the direction of Duane Thomas. Beryl Simon executed the illustrations. The respondents to the survey made by far the largest collective contribution to its accomplishment. They gave freely of their time and knowledge, and thereby gave the research its substance.

CONTENTS

LIST OF FIGURES

Income Equity Among U.S. Workers

CHAPTER

1

FRAMEWORK AND STRATEGY

This book is concerned with how the existing distribution of income affects people's sense of income equity or deprivation, and how these perceptions of distributional equity in turn affect economic behavior. Three personal interview surveys, of representative cross sections of U.S. adults, were conducted in the fall of 1973, of 1974, and 1975, by the Survey Research Center at The University of Michigan. In each survey, workers were questioned about whether they felt they had a fair share of financial rewards; specifically, how they rated their earnings in comparison to what other workers earned, and how satisfactory they found their current family income and standard of living.

This study had two major objectives. First, on what do people base their sense of interpersonal equity or claims of relative deprivation? It is important to determine what these criteria are because they tell us how individual economic circumstance is translated into a personal sense of distributional equity. Moreover, people's distributional preferences, which implicitly underpin such interpersonal income comparisons, are themselves of interest since they can act as guidelines for public policy.

The second objective was to examine how people's sense of distributional equity affects subsequent economic behavior. At the level of individual action, productivity at the workplace and work motivations, as well as dispositions toward collective action in order to redress perceived wage inequity, can be expected to be responsive to relative income comparisons. In addition, since the egalitarian standard often requires nonmarket based distributional methods, equity notions can also be expected to affect citizen preferences for federal income subsidy programs.

In short, this book explores the links between income distribution, sensed interpersonal equity or deprivation, and consequent economic behavior aimed at distributional change. The notion that distributional preferences both help explain and justify the existing distribution is central to this investigation because it implies that distributional preferences contain both descriptive and normative propositions. Polity and economy are here entwined as these relative income evaluations both reflect social welfare preferences, and signal underlying behavioral predispositions toward distributional change.

To feel inequitably treated, people are not simply dissatisfied with their income, but also feel that they are being unjustly denied an increased income share. Differences in their perceptions of interpersonal wage equity, as well as differences in reported satisfactions with family income and living standards, were documented in three independent national samples of working adults. From these data, an initial reading of how people view their comparative economic position emerged, and enabled a more complete view of economic well-being. These data serve as important indicators of economic well-being among working Americans during the 1973-75 period.

To find that unfavorable interpersonal wage comparisons affect economic well-being, however, borders on the tautological. This study therefore investigated the underlying determinants of the income-comparison process itself: do workers feel inequitably treated because they make less than others with equal skills, education, abilities, and seniority? Or do they feel inequitably treated because they have not received salary increases as large as those of other workers? Do the same conditions that embitter one part of the population leave another segment indifferent? Relative income evaluations are multifaceted; their major dimensions were detailed and subjected to empirical analysis to determine the relative importance of these various evaluative criteria.

The second objective of analysis was to determine how sensed income deprivation affects behavioral choice. Here analysis moved beyond the examination of the welfare aspects of distribution, to the motivational content of sensed deprivation; from how the existing distribution affects individual well-being, to how these comparative evaluations act to shape subsequent distributions. Unfavorable income evaluations were expected to promote behavior directed toward the source of income inequity and to be focused on change. That an individual may desire but be unable to effect distributional change is clear. Nonetheless, voiced preferences for federal income, housing, and medical care subsidies may reflect these income evaluations, and thus act to shape public policies that alter the distribution of income.

In addition, individual behavior aimed either at increasing income shares for given work inputs, or decreasing inputs for the same level of income will act to bolster relative wages. Analysis therefore investigated some characteristic types of labor market orientations that act to compensate for felt income loss or press for added advantage. In particular, analysis focused on differences in dispositions toward becoming individually less productive through reduction in effort, prolonged rest breaks, and irregularity of attendance; or by participation in group efforts to increase incomes, such as strikes or protests. Such links not only tell us something of how distribution affects preferences underlying labor inputs supplied at the existing terms of exchange, but also tell of how the market rules or terms of exchange are themselves affected.

FOCUS OF INQUIRY

In this study, establishing the link between income equity and consequent behavioral choice was taken as an object of analytic inquiry. Motives other than those centered on distributional equity were introduced into analysis and contrasted. One such alternate view represented an approach close to the spirit of neoclassical models that exclude distributional considerations directly, yet take some account of relative status considerations. According to this view, interpersonal comparisons are taken as merely one aspect of income evaluations; by themselves, they are not seen as potent motivators of economic behavior nor as prime determinants of well-being. In this view it is not distributional equity, but income position, that counts: low income, no matter the sense of distributional equity, prompts such dispositions toward income change under study.

A second contrasting view takes evaluations of income change, not level, as the basis for evaluation and behavioral response. Norms of distributional equity were still assumed to influence income comparisons, but behavioral responses were seen as more dependent on what patterns of income change people considered fair or appropriate. Since distributional goals are neither easily nor quickly attainable, a sense of income progress may enable much current inequity to be endured without resentment agitation for change. Accordingly, as long as income change was judged consistent with distributional goals, income level inequalities lack behavioral consequence. Here, past income change and expected future gain are what count, not relative level.

A third issue, more methodological in nature, concerns the role of subjective reports of income equity. Whether actual income differences or subjective assessments were better indicators of distributional equity was not at issue as much as whether subjective evaluations had an independent effect on behavior. That is, apart from differences that could be accounted for by actual income position, did subjective income evaluations play a significant role in shaping subsequent behavior aimed at distributional change? Because changes in subjective income evaluations may be more volatile than changes in the underlying income distribution, these assessments may serve as important channels for discontent.

Conceptual Model

The model guiding this analysis is summarized in Figure 1.1. In the center of the figure, the prominent role of economic and social norms governing

FIGURE 1.1

Conceptual Model

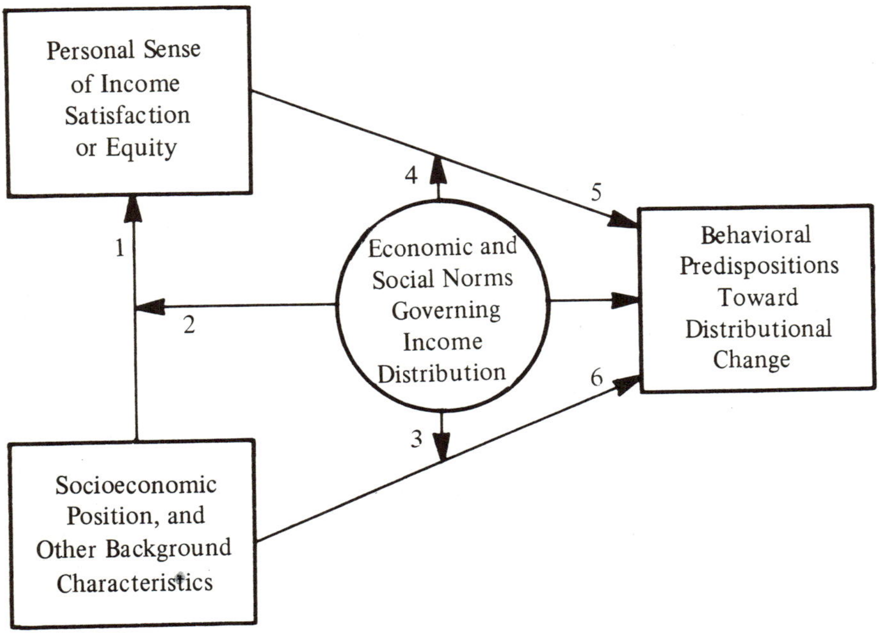

income distribution is highlighted. They not only affect how economic circumstance is translated into a personal sense of equity, but also how relative economic position is translated into predispositions toward distributional change. Between economic circumstance and consequent behavioral reactions, this model interposed subjective income evaluations. They serve to channel and motivate income redress. This model also recognized that predispositions toward redress may be directly linked with more identifiable and established differences in socioeconomic status. Behavioral predispositions were thus investigated as a function of both objective differences in socioeconomic position, and subjective assessments of these differences. Determining whether, and to what extent, differences in subjective evaluations simply mirror actual income differences, or signify important independent sources of motivation for redress, was a central objective of this study.

The first objective of analysis was concerned with the impact of economic experience on people's sense of distributional equity (arrow 1 in the figure), as modified by the effects of social norms on these income evaluations (arrow 2).

In investigating people's own sense of equity, and the factors on which they based their evaluations, it was found that distributional norms did intervene in the evaluation of income differences; unequal incomes were not held inherently inequitable. This analysis revealed that the vast majority of Americans believe that some inequality is justified by individual merit or special circumstance. Such income differentials have long been held crucial for maintaining high levels of work motivation and productivity. Income differentials, moreover, themselves bespeak personal accomplishment, for which social recognition is itself often sought as reward. Finally, analysis revealed that there are limits on the degree of income inequality people believe acceptable regardless of differences in productive inputs.

Next, analysis investigated how individual attitudes and social norms govern the process of distributional change (arrows 3 and 4). Individual behavior is shaped, and the range of acceptable actions is limited, by social norms that regulate conduct in wage disputes. Since claims of inequity are most often based on current outcomes of so-called legitimate processes and institutions, the range of actions studied must include what, from one viewpoint or another, may be considered illegitimate tactics to gain income concessions. More importantly, such a wide range of actions was of interest for this study because such illegitimate tactics, if undertaken, are likely to have repercussions on societal integration and stability, and hence on aggregate economic prospects. Do people have the right to strike, regardless of circumstance? Are they justified in disrupting production—of goods or services, private or public—by work slowdowns, wildcat strikes, being less productive, or doing work poorly or incorrectly on purpose? Should workers' protests that disrupt public order be tolerated? Respondents were directly questioned as to the appropriateness of several such responses to wage inequity. Analysis demonstrated that generally people conform to established rules of conduct, even across lines of economic interests, but that there nonetheless exists a widespread potential for the use of nonmarket strategies to achieve income redress.

Following this, analysis turned to an examination of the desired role of the federal government in the income allocation process, focusing on proposed public policies that would subsidize individual incomes and living standards. Subsidies to individuals and groups, regulation of markets and industries, and the setting of fair conditions of employment and promotion, are all intended to promote a more equitable distribution of income. Should the federal government directly intervene and establish a system of job and standard of living guarantees for all, or should each individual compete on his own, trading his own inputs for what rewards he can command in the marketplace? Should medical care and housing be provided to all at public expense? The answers respondents gave when questioned about these issues are of special interest because these normative criteria not only serve as guidelines for individual behavior, but can also serve as guidelines for public policy. These data indicated that although there was widespread agreement among American workers on the role of federal subsidies, neither complete individual nor government responsibility for providing jobs, housing, and health care was advocated. Instead, more of a middle course was indicated, with major differences in overall preferences being related to the form of subsidy.

Finally, analysis investigated the effects of people's sense of income equity or deprivation (arrow 5) and of their relative income position (arrow 6) on dispositions toward change. Inequity not only conveys a sense of dissatisfaction with income, but also implies that an increased income share is felt to be unjustly denied. People who sense relative deprivation can therefore be expected to more frequently voice concern over their income position and more willingly endorse remedial action, on their own part as well as by groups representing their interests. Analysis identified the underlying socioeconomic characteristics and subjective income evaluations that prompt these heightened concerns for relative income improvement. There, analysis documented that both the more objective characteristics of people's economic circumstances, as well as subjective income evaluations, have significant and independent effects on dispositions toward distributional change.

Methodology

It should be clear that this analysis framework does not, in any way, draw on a normative theory of income distribution. Rather, it is intended to provide a descriptive outline of the effects of income distribution on the well-being of individuals and on behavioral choice. No criterion is proposed by which the observed income distribution can be judged in terms of its welfare content. Interpersonal comparisons of well-being, as made by an independent observer, were not included in analysis. People's judgments of their own economic well-being are documented, although when making such judgments, it is recognized that people, themselves, make use of some social comparison process. But by doing so, no normative judgments that are not already inherent in the Paretian criterion, a long established cornerstone of welfare economics, were incorporated into analysis. Although research in welfare economics has several methodological limitations, the empirical research design utilized was fully in the tradition of positive economic inquiry.

Economic theory, even though welfare interdependencies and interpersonal comparisons are eschewed in formal models, offered substantial guidance for this investigation, both in matters of substance and methodology. The determination of wage income and its changes have long received much analytic attention. Relative income considerations and the role of externalities in consumption and production have also held prominent positions in economic analysis. More recently, income distribution has been examined as a public good, for which privately held preferences serve as indicators of public demand in much the same manner as citizens' preferences for other social programs. Moreover, extensive contributions by welfare theorists have established a methodological foundation which delineates its normative aspects from those amenable to positive study. But much remains unknown. Accordingly this study was exploratory in nature.

Of greatest methodological consequence for the conceptual model guiding this research effort was a matter of perspective: analyses were based on a dynamic view of well-being, more concerned with the process of disequilibrium adjustment than the state of equilibrium rest. One equilibrium state was not contrasted with another to ascertain impacts on well-being. Comparative statistics have little relevance for analyses of distributional equity, as no scientific methodology enables such comparisons of economic well-being. What makes for high levels of well-being today, may be rightly held unsatisfactory tomorrow, without any inconsistency of judgment.

In this inquiry, economic well-being was viewed as the outcome of a dynamic interdependent system. It is dependent on the capacity of the economy to accommodate the demands and preferences of the people, and on the capacity of the people to adapt to their economic situation. Such an analytic focus may well prove more instructive in these times of rapid economic change, especially when potential distributional conflicts threaten to exacerbate existing economic problems, both within and between nations.

Organizational Plan

As its core, this study parts from traditional models of economic behavior by examining how people's sense of well-being and behavior are affected by the amount of income others receive in addition to their own income. The study therefore begins with a brief review of the theoretical development of welfare economics, and of how this development fostered the opinion that, in matters of distributional policy, positive economic analysis had little of substance to offer. But what could not be discounted, regardless of the inherent normative character of distributional issues, was that questions of distribution remain central to both the economic relationships among individuals and the interaction of the functional components of the economy. This represents the often-stated distinction between the size distribution among income classes and distribution of product according to factor shares—which parallels the distinction between concerns for interpersonal equity in the allocation of income and economic efficiency in the use of resources. Consequently, the major aim of Chapter 3 is to elaborate a conceptual model that systematically incorporates the effects of people's interdependence in economic affairs. In doing so, several issues involving the methodology of welfare analysis were also examined.

Chapter 4 reports on the operationalization of this conceptual framework. Several survey measures of people's sense of equity are introduced, and responses tabulated for each survey sample as a whole, and for major population subgroups. Replicated measurement provides a firm foundation to assess reported differences in perceptions of income equity within various segments of the population, and the stability of these reported evaluations over time.

To establish the necessary framework for the subsequent empirical investigation, Chapter 5 more thoroughly delineates and scrutinizes potential determinants of comparative income evaluations. In particular, empirical estimates of income deprivation are developed, based on reported income levels adjusted for differences in individual skills and ability, as well as for differences in normative standards. The multivariate analysis model developed in Chapter 6 then systematically investigates the hypothesized determinants of subjective income evaluations. Since repeated independent observations were utilized to test these models, analysis identified those sources that exerted a systematic and lasting influence, and those that either depended on changing economic circumstance, and thus vary over time, or exhibited only a weak and temporary association.

Chapters 7 and 8 then investigate the link between perceptions of distributional equity and economic choice. The first of these chapters focuses on the normative rules of behavior that place boundaries on tactics that are socially permissible to exact distributional change, and on government subsidies that are advocated as proper. These same social norms also serve to justify undertaking behavior aimed at income redress. The multivariate model in Chapter 8 examines the underlying sources that prompt efforts toward distributional change. In this analysis, the motivational content of people's sense of income equity was of prime concern.

In the final chapter, the results from each of these several analyses are gathered, and their policy implications explored. Since distributional change is inherently a process of disequilibrium adjustment, societal integration and economic stability become crucial aspects of policy choice. Public policy must accommodate privately held distributional preferences, since people's sense of economic justice cannot for long be suppressed in a democratic society that depends on a basic cohesion of interests among its members.

CHAPTER

2

WELFARE ECONOMICS

SOCIAL WELFARE CRITERIA

Defining Economic Justice

The search for a definition of economic justice, one that both commands wide public acceptance and provides practical policy guidance, has motivated much economic analysis. As A. C. Pigou noted long ago, "the goal sought is to make more easy practical measures to promote welfare–practical measures which the statesman may build upon the work of the economist."[1] But the search by economists largely ended with Abram Bergson's now classic statement of the social welfare function, which isolated and identified the role of ethical judgments in economic analysis.[2] His analysis concisely demonstrated that the conditions for the distribution of welfare–distributional equity–are separable from those conditions containing the rules for ideal output–economic efficiency.[3] The view that no positive economic statements could be made about interpersonal equity was henceforth established.[4]

Of course Bergson was not the first to note this separation of economic efficiency from equity. John Stuart Mill clearly recognized this division, and also held that the distribution of income was a matter of social choice, not economic science.[5] And Lionel Robbins, at about the same time that Bergson's work appeared, published his *Essay on the Nature and Significance of Economic Science*, which discredits the use of efficiency criteria and the principle of diminishing marginal utility of income as scientific bases for distributional analysis.[6]

Social Welfare

From this theoretical foundation, two interrelated trends in economic thought took root. First, the so-called New Welfare Economics promoted and firmly established the idea that problems of social welfare are reducible into those which take as their concern individual welfare and those which center on distribution, and that these issues could and should be treated separately. Furtehrmore, since problems of distribution focus on interpersonal-welfare comparisons on which no scientific statements can be made, distributional choice was thought rightly left to political processes for resolution. The domain of welfare economics, more importantly, was thus thought to be meaningfully restricted and yet still enable rigorous analysis of unaggregated individual welfare through the concept of Pareto optimality.[7]

The recognition that normative judgments need to be made separate and distinct from positive economic analysis, however, does not preclude the crucial function attributed to these interpersonal comparisons. As Lester Thurow has noted, "such intellectual conclusions neither obviate the need to make decisions about economic equity nor stop such decisions from being made."[8] Economic policy cannot be neutral with regard to distribution–not when properly examined for its normative implications. For even if policies were designed to leave the existing distribution unchanged, these policies nonetheless clearly express a distinct distribution preference, and hence subsume some aggregate judgment on interpersonal comparisons.

All judgments on redistribution policy necessarily involve interpersonal comparisons. Individuals as well as groups make these decisions all the time. As such, these distributional preferences can be sensibly studied and documented through population surveys.[9] Lee Rainwater has shown that these preferences are susceptible to empirical research in his analysis of changing popular conceptions of adequate living standards. He analyzed data from 18 cross-sectional surveys, covering the period from 1946 through 1969, which asked respondents, "What is the smallest amount of money a family of four needs to get along in this community?" In 1971 dollars, the mean response ranged from $88.75 in 1946 to $132.26 in 1969. However, this amount represented an almost constant 50 percent of family disposable income, and 75 percent of median family income over this entire period.[10] These data indicate that population surveys can provide systematic and robust data for the analyses of distributional equity.

This study does not argue that it is possible, in principle, to aggregate individually held distributional preferences in any sort of scientific manner. Yet an understanding of these preferences, both from an individual viewpoint and societal perspective, is essential for choosing among alternate policies to achieve a desired income and wealth distribution. Thus it is not so much that the division between equity in distribution and efficiency in production is erroneous, but that economic analysis based on this division also proves to be devoid of practical policy guidance.

Individual Welfare

The second trend involves the delineation of the determinants of individual welfare; in particular, the role that the assumption of independent utilities (preferences) played in its development. While the assumption of independence of utilities does impart greatly needed theoretical order to the otherwise vast complexity of human behavior, this assumption can also be seen to render models of economic behavior devoid of much of their motivational content.[11] Utility, in the work of Eugen Slutsky, came to merely signify an unobservable magnitude that was theoretically useful to postulate as a basis for choice, not welfare content.[12] Furthermore, traditional theory holds only that welfare derives in part from some set of economic magnitudes. Nothing is said about how judgments about welfare arise or how they change. But that is the essence of the welfare problem when utilities are interdependent.

Moreover, this assumption of independence has had the unintended side effect of insulating certain aspects of economic welfare from analysis; namely, those aspects of individual well-being whose fulfillment is inherently social rather than individual in nature, as is people's sense of distributional equity. People must make interpersonal comparative evaluations of their position on such welfare dimensions; no other assessment is as salient.

Distributional equity then is necessarily conceptualized as a collective good. This is so because the distribution of income is a characteristic of a collective of people, not of any individual member. All individuals face the same distribution; exclusion is impossible.[13] Furthermore, just as individual preferences cannot be aggregated to establish a unique preference ordering for the group as a whole, distributional equity cannot be meaningfully disaggregated.[14] Distributional equity is thus more than the aggregate of the well-being of individuals taken in parallel. Consequently, provisions for distributional equity that represent a social optimum cannot be induced from individually held distributional preferences.

But this is no cause for the despair often engendered by the impossibility of a direct mapping of individual preferences to a unique social ordering. It only points to the difficulties encountered when individual preferences need to be reconciled with the public interest—a predicament all too consistent with reality in the political economy. While some have proposed "social contract" schemes to enable a reconciliation of private and public interest, this study does not enter such areas of social philosophy.[15] Rather than proposing distributional ideals, it takes the view that the existing distribution is, by design, responsive to both the workings of the invisible hand of the marketplace and to the more visible mechanisms of private and public power. Visible or not, these mechanisms depend on normative approval (or at least acquiescence) in democratic societies. As such, the existing income distribution is subject to modification from changes in normative evaluations, stemming in part from interpersonal comparisons and preferences based on current distributive patterns. Viewed in this manner, private preferences for public goods–in this case, income distribution–serve as indicators for economic policy in much the same way as privately held preferences for expenditure and tax programs.[16]

These trends in economic thought, together with the inherent methodological problems in welfare analysis, promoted little empirical research concerned with how patterns of distribution are translated into subjective feelings of equity or deprivation, and how these relative-income evaluations in turn influence individual and collective behavior aimed at adjusting the prevailing income distribution. In short, the analysis of distributional preferences and their effect on economic choice has long been neglected. As Harold Hochman has said, "That economists can have much to say about distributional matters is not so nearly surprising as its history of neglect."[17]

The next chapter details a conceptual model to guide such an empirical investigation of relative-income evaluations. The analytic framework proposed is not free of ethical assumptions, nor can it be. In essence, this model accepts the primacy of an individual's own evaluation of his economic circumstances. It will not be based, however, on independence of preferences, nor separability of productive efficiency from distributional equity. Indeed, it is the investigation of these underlying interrelationships that was in part the focus of this inquiry.

Considering the complexity of the phenomenon under investigation, population survey measures that focus directly on the evaluative outcomes of interpersonal income comparisons, not just on observed income differentials, hold much promise as policy indicators. This approach offers much in terms of welfare content, and has substantial appeal on methodological grounds as well, since respondents were directly questioned about their own sense of income equity or relative deprivation. But before we can accept people's sense of distributional equity based on survey items as the basic datum or welfare criterion for analysis, questions of methodology and research design must be carefully explored.

RESEARCH METHODOLOGY

Economic Well-Being

Economic well-being is a concept that seemingly defies empirical analysis. Although changes in welfare are clearly perceived by individuals, welfare change is neither interpersonally comparable nor quantifiable over time. Because individual well-being cannot be impartially observed, "the end to which the analysis is adapted is not empirically given to the investigator; it is instead postulated by the investigator."[18] Statements on welfare change are therefore unlike positive propositions in economics, since they are not susceptible to direct empirical tests. We must either accept or reject some particular definition of an improvement in individual welfare on the basis of normative judgment. No objective test is possible. "It is clear that the interest attaching to a theory of welfare depends almost entirely upon the realism and relevance of its assumptions, factual and ethical, in a particular historical context."[19]

Positive economic theory is based on a set of axioms or assumptions. Empirical tests are concerned with the validity of the theoretical implications; the validity of the assumptions themselves is of no direct concern. Rather, interest is focused on the correspondence of the implied empirical predictions with unfolding economic events. In the case of welfare propositions, however, a direct test of the theoretical implications for individual well-being is, if at all possible, more difficult than a direct test of the assumptions on which these predictions rest. This is opposite to the case of positive propositions.[20] Whereas in positive economics, as Johannes de V. Graaff observes, "the proof of the pudding is indeed in the eating. The welfare cake, on the other hand, is so hard to taste that we must . . . scrutinize with care and thoroughness each assumption."[21] Consequently, a methodology that attempts to ascertain the validity of the assumptions themselves, rather than their derived theoretical implications, is needed. If the assumptions about economic motivations and behavior are correct, and the delineation of the economic correlates of welfare are accurate, and if no other considerations are relevant, then the application of good rules of logic insures that the theoretical implications for changes in individual well-being will follow from these premises.[22]

An unwillingness to accept these methodological constraints on scientific inquiry has led some to the position that analysis must restrict itself to a positive study of how some arbitrary, but interesting welfare index responds to various economic variables and institutional arrangements. The use of real income as an index of economic welfare is the most often used proxy of this type. But these problems of methodology remain just as before. Inferences drawn from changes in objective measures still require the force of normative judgment rather than resting alone on results from positive analysis.

Consider, for example, measures of inequality of income shares as documented by the Lorenz curve and the Gini Index of Concentration. The Lorenz curve shows the cumulated fraction of aggregate income plotted against the cumulated proportion of individuals, when individuals are arrayed in ascending order by income. The index of concentration represents the proportionate area between the curve and the diagonal that signifies complete equality. The index ranges from zero, indicating complete equality of shares, to one, for extreme inequality. But how should such numerical indices be interpreted? Are we to assume strict equality of income shares is most desirable for maximum social welfare, regardless of relative inputs or productive efficiency? Or is it more socially preferred that rewards be distributed in proportion to input to attain maximum social welfare? According to the latter assumption, the realized value of the Gini coefficient (and its changes over time) needs to be contrasted not with equality, but with the corresponding distribution of inputs, such as indicated by a Lorenz curve of the cumulative distribution of abilities and skills within a given society.[23] Here, particular Gini values have meaning only in relation to the prevailing input distribution. Moreover, in either case, that which represents greater social welfare cannot be determined by simple inspection, nor by complex statistical technique. Normative judgments are still required to interpret changes in these objective measures.

Population Surveys

Welfare then is necessarily subjective; it properly refers to the experiences of individuals. Jeremy Bentham, in commenting on social welfare theory in the eighteenth century, enunciated "the greatest happiness principle." Pigou, in *The Economics of Welfare*, states that "the true elements of welfare are states of consciousness."[24] That welfare is "a state of mind" is widely accepted.[25] In this study, empirical analyses are based on data generated from population sample surveys, which questioned respondents as to their own perceptions of income equity or deprivation (see the Appendix for details on sample design and interviewing). People's voiced preferences and interpersonal evaluations were interpreted as accurate reflections of that which was most conducive to their own welfare. The implied research design thus accepted that each individual is the best judge of their own well-being, an assumption not subject to empirical verification. This design does not, in any manner, open the theoretical basis of analysis to criticisms of consumer irrationality, or nonconsistency, nor is it in any way a frivolous criterion of welfare change. It would, however, be a mistake to assume that such voiced preferences are at all times plausible. People's perceptions of distributional equity were therefore accorded hypothesis status. In so doing, primary emphasis was placed not on accepting people's notions of equity as a consequence of an ethical judgment, but, rather, as a consequence of our interest in distributional equity itself.

As Graaff says, "we shall try to maintain an element of objectivity by linking individual welfare very closely to individual choice."[26] This inquiry attests to that view by maintaining a dual concern for both the welfare content and behavioral consequences of people's notions of income equity. Distinguishing self-seeking envy and idle compassion from that which affects economic choice was an essential feature of the research design. This investigation of distributional equity thus finds methodological warrant in its attempt to demonstrate a correspondence between people's sense of income equity and consequent economic behavior.

NOTES

1. A. C. Pigou, *The Economics of Welfare*, 4th ed. (London: Macmillan, 1960), p. 10.

2. Abram Bergson, "A Reformulation of Certain Aspects of Welfare Economics," *Quarterly Journal of Economics* 52 (February 1938): 310-34.

3. Ezra J. Mishan, "A Survey of Welfare Economics, 1939-1959," *Economic Journal* 70 (June 1960): 197-265. In order to separate efficiency from equity, the following ethical judgments were accepted by Bergson: (1) each individual–and no one else–is the best judge of his own well-being; (2) the welfare of the community, as a whole, depends on the welfare of the individuals comprising it, and on nothing else; (3) if at least one person is better off, no one being worse off, the community may be said to be better off. Social welfare functions of the Bergson-Samuelson type, in their general form, are mathematical expressions whose parameters are shaped by assumptions 1 and 2 above. On this see Paul A. Samuelson, *Foundations of Economic Analysis* (Cambridge: Harvard University Press, 1947), chap. 8. Both these ethical judgments are implicit in the construction of the utility possibility frontier, which is the maximum or outer boundary of all utility combinations possible with the given resources of the economy. The third judgment refers to the familiar definition of Pareto improvements. As such, it constitutes a widely acceptable welfare criterion of limited applicability; it does not enable comparisons when, as is most always the case, some are made better off, some worse off by changes in distribution.

4. It should be noted that the conclusion that no positive economic statements can be made about equity is simply a matter of logic, not economics; ethical judgments cannot be deduced from purely factual studies. Also, note that statements about economic efficiency are not value free. They depend on an underlying set of identifiable (and discussable) value judgments. For example, Pareto optimality, in addition to the above noted value judgments (see note 3), also accepts that more of a scarce resource is better, and a greater range of economic choice is better. It thus incorporates a progrowth philosophy of political economy.

5. John Stuart Mill, *Principles of Political Economy*, ed. J. M. Robson (Toronto: University of Toronto Press, 1965).

6. Lionel Robbins, *An Essay on the Nature and Significance of Economic Science* (London: Macmillan, 1937).

7. Herbert Glintis, "A Radical Analysis of Welfare Economics and Individual Development," *Quarterly Journal of Economics* 86 (November 1972): 572-99.

8. Lester Thurow, "Toward a Definition of Economic Justice," *Public Interest* 31 (Spring 1973): 57.

9. Kenneth E. Boulding, "Love, Fear and the Economist: An Interview," *Challenge* 16 (July/August, 1973): 38.

10. Lee Rainwater, *What Money Buys: Inequality and the Social Meaning of Income* (New York: Basic Books, 1974), p. 53. One omission in Rainwater's analysis was that he discounted the impact of real economic growth on reference standards. Just as income reference standards were invariant with price level changes, reference standards may also be revised to account for real economic growth. This may be the reason these data show an increase in the minimum income level in constant dollars over this time period, as compared to a constant proportion of median income.

11. James S. Duesenberry, *Income, Saving, and the Theory of Consumer Behavior* (Cambridge: Harvard University Press, 1949).

12. Eugen E. Slutsky, "On the Theory of the Budget of the Consumer," in *Readings in Price Theory*, ed. George J. Stigler and Kenneth E. Boulding (Chicago: Irwin, 1952), pp. 27-56.

13. Just as these characteristics signal the public goods character of distribution, they also indicate that "each individual has a vested interest in disguising his preferences concerning his desired income distribution to avoid paying his optimal share of the necessary transfer payments." Lester C. Thurow, "The Income Distribution as a Pure Public Good," *Quarterly Journal of Economics* 85 (May 1971): 329.

14. Kenneth J. Arrow, *Social Choice and Individual Values*, 2d ed. (New York: Wiley, 1963).

15. John Rawls, for example, argues that there is only one distribution of rewards that everyone would be willing to accept: the reward structure that maximizes the minimum reward. See his *A Theory of Justice* (Cambridge: Harvard University Press, 1971). The same type of framework was earlier outlined by John Harsanyi in "Cardinal Utility in Welfare Economics and the Theory of Risk Taking," *Journal of Political Economy* 61 (October 1953): 434-35. See also James M. Buchanan and Gordon Tullock, *The Calculus of Consent* (Ann Arbor: University of Michigan Press, 1965).

16. For an analysis of individually held preferences for various fiscal policies, see Richard T. Curtin and Charles D. Cowan, "Public Attitudes Toward Fiscal Programs," in *Surveys of Consumers 1972-73: Contributions to Behavioral Economics*, ed. Burkhard Strumpel et al. (Ann Arbor: Institute for Social Research, University of Michigan, 1975).

17. Harold M. Hochman, "Individual Preferences and Distributional Adjustments," *American Economic Review* 62 (May 1972): 360.

18. Jerome Rothenberg, *The Measurement of Social Welfare* (New York: Prentice-Hall, 1961), p. 4.

19. Johannes de V. Graaff, *Theoretical Welfare Economics* (Cambridge, England: Cambridge University Press, 1957), p. 3.

20. Note, however, that these problems of methodology do not constitute a very serious criticism of welfare economics as a scientific discipline. See Ezra J. Mishan, *Welfare Economics: An Assessment*, (Amsterdam: North-Holland, 1969), pp. 13-22.

21. On this see ibid.

22. On this see ibid.

23. On this topic see Harold Lydall, *The Structure of Earnings* (Oxford, England: Clarendon Press, 1968), chap. 2 and 7.

24. Pigou, op. cit., p. 10.

25. See, for example, Graaff, op. cit., and Mishan, "A Survey of Welfare Economics, 1939-1959," op. cit. It should be noted that this view implies that people's well-being cannot be sensibly partitioned into that which is economic welfare and that part which is non-economic. As I. M. D. Little points out: "There is no part of well-being called 'economic well-being.' The word 'economic' qualified not well-being, but the causes of well-being or changes in it. If I am interested only in someone's economic welfare, then I interest myself only in the economic things which may affect his well-being." *A Critique of Welfare Economics*, 2d ed. (Oxford, England: Oxford University Press, 1957), p. 6.

26. Graaff, op. cit., p. 5. For similar reasons, Pigou restricted the range of his inquiry "to that part of social welfare that can be brought directly or indirectly into relation with the measuring-rod of money." Op. cit., p. 18. In a more recent statement of this same guiding principle, Little finds the economic causes of changes in the well-being of individuals "to be those things and services which the individual consumes or enjoys, and which could be exchanged for money, together with the amount and kind of work which the individual does." Op. cit., p. 6. In a similar fashion Graaff and Kelvin J. Lancaster, among others,

linked the economic causes of changes in well-being to expansion of people's area of economic choice. See Lancaster, "A New Approach to Consumer Theory," *Journal of Political Economy* 74 (April 1966): 132-57. Viewed in this manner, "a person's welfare map is defined to be identical with his preference map" and is coupled with the assumption that, given the opportunity to make a choice, people will choose that which enhances their welfare. Graaff, op. cit., p. 5.

CHAPTER

3

DISTRIBUTIONAL PREFERENCES

THEORETICAL MODEL

Assumptions

The theoretical model (highlighted in Chapter 1) views the determination of income distribution as part of the overall economic process, and dependent on the interrelationships of individual welfare functions on the one hand, and production functions on the other. For a given population, with existing technology and available resources, increasing the equality of incomes may entail lower overall income levels in the future, if, as has long been suspected, the lessening of financial incentives reduces productive efficiency. Because of this concern over both equity and efficiency, individuals are assumed to hold preferences concerning the distribution of income.

To systematically investigate these distributional preferences, a partial analysis framework was utilized to isolate and clarify the role of individually held preferences. It has been postulated and extensively relied upon in welfare analysis that changes in the economic causes of welfare will be consistently translated into actual changes in well-being in the same qualitative direction; for example, that changes in overall well-being are at least a nondecreasing function of an index of economic choice expansion. Given, however, that overall welfare is only partially dependent on economic causes, welfare analysis must proceed on the assumption that the noneconomic causes remain unchanged or only vary within certain prescribed limits. Noneconomic determinants of well-being constitute exogenous variables in welfare analysis; they can influence the economic variables but may not be influenced by them.[1]

Individual Welfare Function

For this analysis, individual well-being is taken to depend on the level of one's own income, and on the income position of others, the appropriate concept being the discounted future stream of all income, of which present market earnings are only a part. This may be symbolized as

$$W_i = f_i (Y_i , Y_j),$$

where W_i represents the welfare position, and Y_i the level of income of the ith individual. The subscript j reflects the inclusion of distributional considerations, and is intended to delineate some set (vector) of income comparison referents, not of some specific person; more fully, the vector of all other incomes.[2] The functional notation f_i signifies that the relationship between income and well-being is not the same for everyone; rather, it is a matter of individual judgment. In addition, the relationship between changes in income and welfare is assumed to be ordinal in character (the scales by which both welfare and income are measured are arbitrary in everything except order), meaning that each additional dollar does not necessarily yield equal increments in well-being—interpersonally or intrapersonally. This model thus does not rely on empirical representations of cardinal (interpersonally comparable) utility; it is neither necessary nor appropriate for the analysis of interpersonal evaluations of well-being. Rather, attention is focused on preference or choice, as affected by income and its distribution.

Distributional Impacts

How does the distribution of income affect individual well-being? How do changes in others' income affect one's own well-being? It is postulated that the impact of relative income evaluations on well-being is dependent on the level of others' income at which the interdependence is evaluated. That is, comparative income evaluations are taken to be dependent on the relative position occupied by the jth individual in the overall distribution of income. This postulate is shown diagrammatically in Figure 3.1. Plotted there is one's own welfare (W_i) as a function of others' income(Y_j), while one's own income (Y_i) remains constant. At very low levels of income, marginal increases in others' income act to increase one's own well-being. On the other extreme, further increases in what are already considered high incomes lead to a lessened sense of well-being. Between these extremes lies that which people judge to be an optimum level of others' income, in terms of their own well-being. At its peak, others' incomes are in accordance with their distributional preferences; distributional equity can be said

FIGURE 3.1

The Relationship between People's Own Sense of Welfare and Changes in the Incomes of Others, While Their Own Income Remains Constant

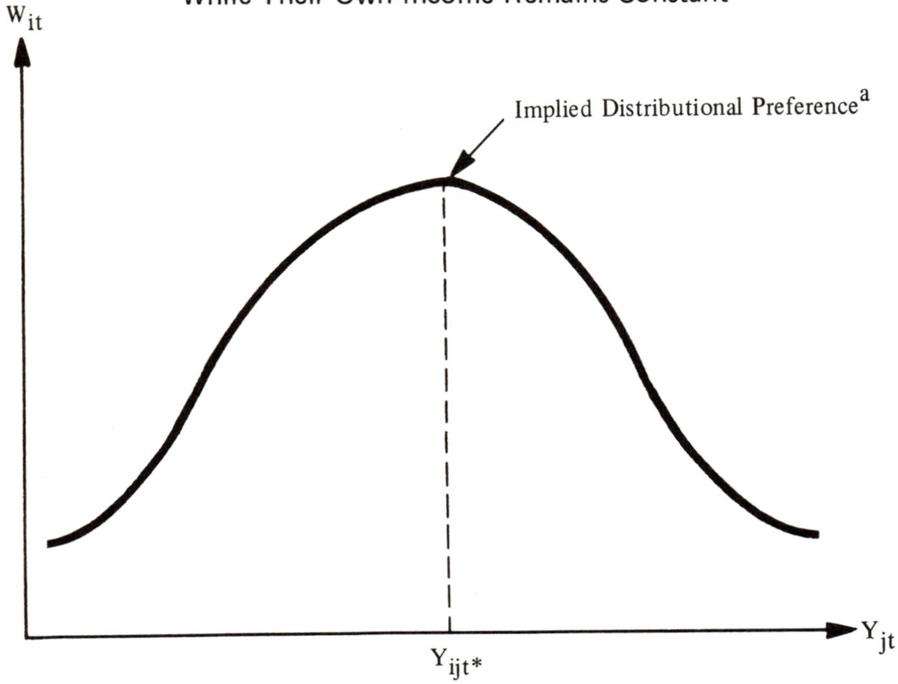

Note: Implied distributional preference refers to the distributional preference of the ith individual for the jth individual's distributive share.

to prevail at this point (in the view of the ith individual with respect to the jth income share). As drawn, the smooth symmetrical shape, as well as the single maximum point, are meant to be illustrative of just one potential array of distributional preferences.

The most common explanation of positive interdependence effects relies on altruistic motivations, expressions of which are common at both the individual and collective level: charity, income maintenance programs, foreign aid, and the like. However, it should be noted that such positive interdependence effects are not just dependent on altruistic motives: favorable income progress made by others is often taken to signal future improvements in one's own income, and thus bolster one's own sense of well-being. Accordingly, income gains made by others are not judged unfavorably when people expect the same increase in their own income.[3] Of course, looking toward income referents for information on one's own future can result in apprehension, rather than encouragement over the gains made by others, and so lessen people's sense of well-being.

The opposite of altruistic motivations are termed egoistic. Here, income increases received by others tend to diminish one's own sense of well-being. As depicted by the right segment of the curve in Figure 3.1, felt well-being responds negatively to marginal increases in Y_j: the more others earn, the greater the sense of deprivation with one's own income. Such negative evaluations, however, as evidenced by greed or envy, are often discounted as being irrelevant to economic analysis.[4] Indeed, it is most often the case, in both theoretical and empirical studies, to restrict analysis to interdependence effects arising from altruistic motives, leaving unfavorable interpersonal comparisons with neither operational meaning nor economic consequence.[5] In this study, all interpersonal comparisons are considered relevant whenever their presence generates any desire on the part of those affected, positively or negatively, to modify the behavior of those responsible either through trade, persuasion, or collective action.[6] The necessary distinction thus being made is between self-seeking envy or idle compassion from that which affects economic choice.

Until now only the general form of the relationship between individual well-being and distributive shares has been postulated. A more detailed specification is needed so that an investigation of interpersonal comparisons can be empirically implemented. To do so, this model further posits that the income level at which individual welfare curves are centered provides a basis for empirical classification. While this point is not intended to have a rigorous statistical meaning, it may be considered to represent a central tendency. In Figure 3.1, the welfare curve W_i was drawn such that its maximum was centered at Y_j^*, with the asterisk indicating that this amount serves as an income reference standard.

Particular realized values of Y_j^* are taken to be dependent on the characteristics of the i_{th} individual, and also on the currently prevailing income levels and their associated distribution. A full specification would be symbolized as Y_{ijt}^*: the level of the jth person's income at time t corresponding to the central tendency of the ith individual's welfare curve. Since these maximum points Y_{ijt}^* are defined within the context of a particular individual's welfare function, they can be interpreted as representing individually held distributional preferences. In addition, these same maximum points can also be conceptualized as representing an income referent or standard of comparison. In this sense, well-being is said to be best served when incomes are in accordance with these just standards of rewards. These are not alternative conceptualizations: distributional preferences operationalized are income reference standards.

STANDARDS OF DISTRIBUTIONAL EQUITY

Income Standards

What evaluative standards do people use in making interpersonal income comparisons? These internalized standards of economic justice are the foundation of people's sense of equity or claims of deprivation. In the 1974 *Economic Report of the President*, the following view was set forth: "Three fundamental principles of equity concerning the distribution of income are widely accepted: those who produce the same amount should be rewarded equally; those who produce more should be rewarded more; and no individual or household should be forced to fall below some minimum standard of consumption regardless of productive potential."[7] The first two principles delineate a proportional rule of income distribution: income is to be distributed, not equally, but on an input criterion. The third is more egalitarian, more concerned with unequal incomes regardless of inputs or abilities. This principle acts to set limits on the degree of income inequality deemed acceptable.

These considerations may be formalized as follows: Let Y symbolize the vector of rewards, X the inputs that are relevant for comparison. People's sense of distributional equity is then taken to result from the application of normative rules for the interpersonal comparisons of quantities of the form Y/X.[8] Distributional equity can be said to exist when

$$(Y/X)_i = (Y/X)_j^*,$$

where $(Y/X)_j^*$ is the standard of comparison. That is, an individual perceives his distributional share as equitable when the rewards accorded him are perceived to be in correct proportion to his inputs. Relative deprivation is said to exist when there is a negative imbalance:

$$(Y/X)_i < (Y/X)_j^*.$$

In this situation an individual feels his proportional share of rewards to be less than what distributional justice entitles him. The opposite case, termed relative gratification, is defined by the condition,

$$(Y/X)_i > (Y/X)_j^*.$$

Under this comparison model, differential allocations of rewards are not in themselves deemed inequitable. That is, inequality of work income does not necessarily imply subjective inequity (an unfavorable comparison), as inputs also need to be taken into account. However, if the normative standard equality of rewards is used in making comparative-income evaluations, input differences are discounted and the form of comparison reduces to

$$Y_i \lesseqgtr Y_j^*.$$

Here, relative deprivation is simply the semantic inverse of relative income.

In the more general case, the X vector in the full formulation can be interpreted as a set of subjective weights or adjustments applied to differences in money incomes that enable comparative judgments on income equity. Even under the standard of equality, such adjustments are often needed to take account of interindividual differences in circumstance and need. As Richard Musgrave has noted, even if the criterion of equal welfare shares "is accepted, this does not necessarily require actual equality in the distribution of income, which would follow only if all people are similar in their propensity to enjoy income."[9]

Reference Groups

Further distinctions based on the delineation of referent $(Y/X)_j^*$ may be drawn. First, reference standards may be defined to be solely concerned with within-group comparisons; that is, for example, comparisons among different members of the same occupational group. Here the standard has relevance only in the context of comparisons made between self and others who are members of one's own reference group. Such comparisons are of the form,

$$(Y/X)_i \lesseqgtr (Y/X)_j \text{ (within group)}^*.$$

A second type of referent standard may be defined that addresses comparisons made between one's own input reference group and other groups in society. Here, we refer, for example, to comparisons of distributional shares between occupational groups. This type of evaluation is termed fraternalistic deprivation, equity, or gratification, according to whether

$$(Y/X)_i \lesseqgtr (Y/X)_j \text{ (between groups)}^*,$$

where the subscript i is taken to implicitly define group membership. It has been maintained that perceived group or fraternalistic deprivation, not within-group or individual deprivation, is of direct consequence for perceptions of distributive justice.[10]

Interpersonal Equity

Returning now to the welfare analysis model, it was postulated that the individual welfare curve W_i (see Figure 3.1) may be taken to be centered at some point Y_j^*, whose scale had only ordinal meaning. It can now be further postulated that at point Y_j^* the following condition is (approximately) met:

$$(Y/X)_{jt} = (Y/X)_{ijt}^*,$$

where $(Y/X)_{ijt}^*$ is the referent standard employed by the ith individual in making distributive evaluations with regard to the jth individual's income share. Thus, this point represents a position of distributional equity from the viewpoint of the ith individual. If, however,

$$(Y/X)_{jt} < (Y/X)_{ijt}^*,$$

relative deprivation may be seen to form the basis for negative marginal interdependence effects. That is, if others income were further increased, people's heightened sense of relative deprivation would detract from their own well-being. Similarly, relative gratification can be seen to provide the basis for positive marginal interdependence effects. Figure 3.2 details welfare interdependence in terms of these considerations.

When interpreted in this manner, it is apparent that this model also postulates an analogous relationship with respect to the changes in one's own income and own well-being, while holding constant the incomes of others.* This relationship is depicted in Figure 3.3, showing this symmetry imposed by the condition of consistency in evaluations of relative-income shares, at any one point in time. Accordingly, when one's own income is increased from relatively very low levels while the incomes of others are held constant, it will increase one's own sense of well-being; but after some point further increases in one's own income, at the expense of others, only detract from one's own sense of well-being. Note that the maximum welfare position, at point Y_{it}^*, implicitly defines distributional preferences from the viewpoint of one's own income share, whereas in Figure 3.1 the implied distributional preference was that of the ith individual for the distributive share of the jth person. Note also that the interpretation of relative deprivation/gratification is similarly affected. In the first case, people's sense of interpersonal equity stemmed from changes in others' income, their own income being held constant; whereas here, people's sense of deprivation or

---

*Of course with a fixed amount to distribute, gains in one's own income share are made at the expense of others, so in this sense all other incomes cannot remain constant. Nonetheless, it still proves instructive to elaborate these propositions as if the income gains accruing to any particular individual, even though these gains may well represent a large proportionate change in one's own income, are offset by income losses among others that are spread widely so that no other single individual undergoes a significant proportional reduction in their income share.

FIGURE 3.2

Interpersonal Equity Considerations within the Context of an Individual's Welfare Function

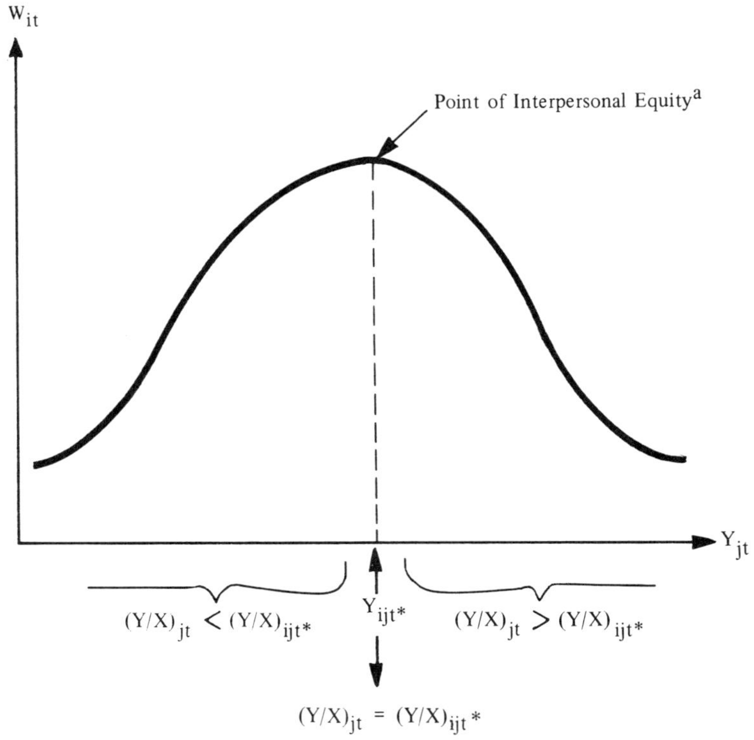

Note: Point of interpersonal equity is from the viewpoint of the ith individual, when comparison is made to j^{th} individual's income.

gratification is prompted by changes in their own income, the income of others being held constant. Finally, it should be stressed that although both points $Y_{ijt}*$ and $Y_{it}*$ represent reference standards on which people base their comparative evaluations, they need not be identical—interpersonally or intrapersonally. It is only in the special case where strict equality of income shares serves as a universal reference standard that these points become identical.

DESCRIPTIVE AND NORMATIVE PROPOSITIONS

The notion that distributional preferences both help explain and justify the existing distribution is important because it implies that distributional

FIGURE 3.3

The Relationship between People's Own Sense of Welfare and Changes in Their Own Income, While the Incomes of Others Remain Constant

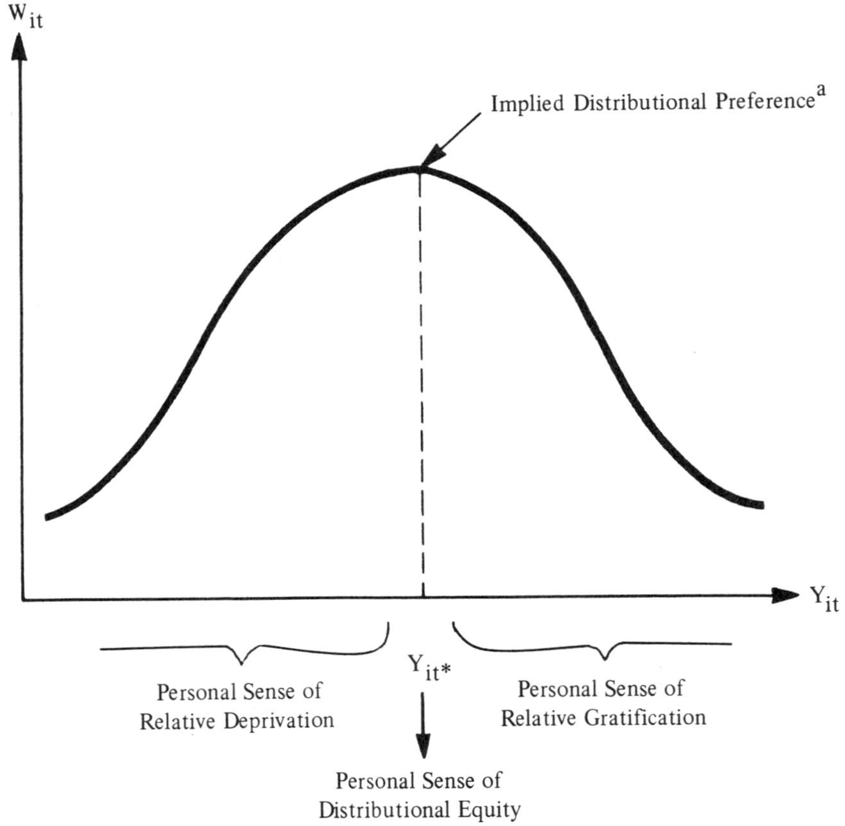

Note: Implied distributional preference refers to the distributional preference of the ith individual for his own distributive share.

preferences contain both empirical and normative propositions; that they not only are descriptive of the political economy, but also of people's evaluation of their own welfare position in relation to others. Likewise, it is important to stress the dual normative character of the concept of equity: It represents a social norm, or rule, on which the distribution of income ought to be based; yet it also encompasses a personal standard by which one may evaluate self in relation to others. Such evaluations enable people to learn about themselves through social comparisons.[11] Relative wage rates, for example, relfect differences in economic productivity, and also represent differences in social evaluation.[12]

In this chapter two distinct standards of distributional equity were outlined that underpin the normative basis for people's judgments of equity or deprivation. They in no sense, however, form alternative hypotheses, as differences in these income standards rest on value judgments, propositions which are not capable of refutation by empirical analysis. They are nonetheless descriptive, and analysis can seek to sort out the relative impacts of these standards on people's sense of distributional equity.

This basic distinction between equal income shares and income in proportion to inputs as distributive criteria is time honored, with many of its facets and implications—both economic and noneconomic—having been often explored. Of particular concern here is how these criteria relate to people's distribution preferences. If incomes are to be distributed on an input basis, distributional equity is usually said to require that risks or opportunities be equalized, whereas if opportunities are uneven and risks substantial, equality of shares may be more often seen as equitable.[13] The difference then in advocating one standard of distribution over another is not just a matter of normative judgment, but also of individual circumstance. For example, an individual who is a risk averter and finds himself in a situation where the potential risks are great, may be reasonably expected to support an equal-share criterion, even if that individual were philosophically opposed to income equality in principle.[14] Moreover, not only the risks of income instability, but also those associated with changing opportunity structures, may lead people to prefer greater income equality. Workers whose skills are no longer in demand, as well as those who find their opportunities unduly constrained, may find practical benefit in equality, whereas input proportionality may be more consonant with their normative judgments.

James D. Rogers examines three theories that try to account for the behavioral motivations underlying observed income redistribution. These models explain redistribution in terms of self-interested behavior on the part of the majority who benefit from redistribution away from the rich, voluntary agreements among individuals to insure themselves against risks, and utility or welfare interdependence.[15] While this investigation is not directly concerned with the insurance model, nor with social contract, constitutional arrangements, or voter coalitions as determinants or mechanisms of redistribution, people's distributional preferences are expected to be influenced by each self-interest, risk, and interdependence. It is to the empirical analysis of these interrelationships to which we now turn.

NOTES

1. A. C. Pigou, in addressing himself to this issue, invoked what he called a "judgement of probability" and asserted "qualitative conclusions about the effect of an economic

cause upon economic welfare will hold good also of the effect on total welfare." Pigou goes on, however, to make some important qualifications: "An economic cause may affect non-economic welfare in ways that cancel its effect on economic welfare." Second, "noneconomic welfare is liable to be modified by the manner in which income is spent. Of different acts of consumption that yield satisfaction, one may exercise a debasing and another an elevating influence." *The Economics of Welfare*, 4th ed. (London: Macmillan, 1960), p. 20. Finally, there may be important differences between social and private valuations. As implied by the above qualifications, increases in "economic welfare" may have perverse effects on the overall well-being of individuals. Still, we have an abiding interest in uncovering and investigating the economic correlates of people's welfare and thus shall make use of the familiar ceterus paribus of economic analysis.

2. Often this delineation of income referents is avoided by resorting to a two-person analysis framework, but much of the flavor of distributional analysis is then lost. On this point see George M. von Furstenberg and Dennis C. Mueller, "The Pareto Optimal Approach to Redistribution: A Fiscal Application," *American Economic Review* 61 (September 1971): 628-37. But for a mathematical development of interdependent preferences in the context of a three-person economy, see James S. Duesenberry, *Income, Saving, and the Theory of Consumer Behavior* (Cambridge: Harvard University Press, 1949), chap. 6.

3. Albert O. Hirschman, "The Changing Tolerance for Income Inequality," *Quarterly Journal of Economics* 87 (November 1973): 544-66.

4. But see Geoffrey Brennan, "Pareto Desirable Redistribution: The Case of Malice and Envy," *Journal of Public Economics* 2 (April 1973): 173-83.

5. For example, Harold Hochman and James Rogers only allow for the possibility of altruism by including the total income of the poor as a determinant of distributional preferences of potential donors. See their "Pareto Optimal Redistribution," *American Economic Review* 59 (September 1969): 542-57. Similarly, Mark Pauly restricts his analysis to commodities consumed by the poor that generate externalities. See his "Optimality, Public Goods, and Local Governments: A General Theoretical Analysis," *Journal of Political Economy* 78 (May/June 1972): 572-85.

6. James M. Buchanan and William C. Stubbebine, "Externality," *Economica* 29 (November 1962): 371-84.

7. *Economic Report of the President* (Washington, D.C.: U.S. Government Printing Office, 1974), p. 137.

8. Economists have long been interested in the concept of equity as it relates to the distribution of public expenditures and taxation. The benefit approach to taxation as opposed to the ability-to-pay criterion has been at the center of economic debate for many centuries. Pigou and, before him, Adam Smith noted both approaches, and 100 years before Smith's *The Wealth of Nations* appeared, Sir William Petty wrote, "it is generally allowed by all that men should contribute to the public charge but according to the share and interest they have in the public peace." "A Treatise on Taxes and Contribution," 1677, in *The Economic Writings of Sir William Petty*, ed. C. H. Hall (Cambridge, England: Cambridge University Press, 1899), p. 91. See Richard A. Musgrave, *The Theory of Public Finance*, (New York: McGraw-Hill, 1959), chaps. 4-5, for a stimulating survey of these developments. There is also an extensive literature on the sociopsychological concept of equity and relative deprivation. See, for example, S. A. Stouffer et al., *The American Soldier: Adjustments During Army Life* (Princeton: Princeton University Press, 1949); J. Stacy Adams, "Injustice in Social Exchange," in *Advances in Experimental Social Psychology*, vol. 2, ed. L. Berkowitz (New York: Academic Press, 1965), pp. 267-99; George C. Homans, *Social Behavior: Its Elementary Forms* (New York: Harcourt, Brance, and World, 1961); Elliott Jacques, *Equitable Payment* (New York: Wiley, 1961); Peter M. Blau, *Exchange and Power in Social Life* (New York: Wiley, 1964); and Thomas F. Pettigrew, "Social Evaluation Theory: Con-

tingencies and Applications," in *Nebraska Symposium on Motivation: 1967*, ed. David Levine (Lincoln: University of Nebraska Press, 1967), pp. 241-311. Homans, for example, formulates distributional justice as follows: "A man in an exchange relationship with another will expect that the rewards of each man be proportional to his costs–the greater the rewards, the greater the costs–and that the net rewards, or profits, of each man be proportional to his investments–the greater the investments, the greater the profit." Op. cit., p. 75.

9. Musgrave, op. cit., p. 9.

10. On this point, see Adams, op. cit.; Pettigrew, op. cit.; and Walter G. Runciman, *Relative Deprivation and Social Justice* (Berkeley: University of California Press, 1966).

11. John W. Thibaut and Harold H. Kelley, *The Social Psychology of Groups* (New York: Wiley, 1959).

12. "The basic tenet of social evaluation theory is that human beings learn about themselves by comparing themselves to others. A second tenet is that the process of social evaluation leads to positive, neutral, or negative self-ratings which are relative to the standards set by the individuals employed for comparison." Pettigrew, op. cit., p. 243.

13. This same distinction between equality of opportunity and equality of outcomes has been conceptualized respectively as ex ante and ex post equity by Mark V. Pauly and Thomas D. Willett, in "Two Concepts of Equity and Their Implications for Public Policy," *Social Science Quarterly* 53 (June 1972): 8-19.

14. See William Breit and William Culbertson, "Distributional Equality and Aggregate Utility: Comment," *American Economic Review* 60 (June 1970): 435-41 and references cited there.

15. James D. Rogers, "Explaining Income Redistribution," in *Redistribution Through Public Choice*, ed. Harold M. Hochman and George E. Peterson (New York: Columbia University Press, 1974), pp. 165-205.

CHAPTER

4

PERCEPTIONS OF INCOME EQUITY

How widespread is the sense of income equity among Americans? Are there significant numbers of workers who feel they get less pay than they deserve? Personal interview surveys of representative cross sections of U.S. adults, conducted in November of 1973, of 1974, and 1975, questioned workers about their own perceptions of income equity or deprivation. This chapter introduces four survey measures of interpersonal equity. Responses were tabulated for several socioeconomic and demographic classifications to gain an initial overview of people's sense of income equity. Analysis was intended to be primarily descriptive and concerned with welfare content of the responses rather than being focused on the underlying determinants of relative income evaluations. The distribution of these responses indicates the extent of perceived income deprivation or equity in the population. In the following chapter, the comparison process itself is analyzed, detailing a multivariate strategy to investigate the bases of these income evaluations.

The secondary aim of this chapter, less explicit in its exposition, was to assess the validity of the survey measurements themselves. Survey questions, to be acceptable, must yield reliable results capable of replication. Repeated measurement of income deprivation or equity should not show random variation beyond known sampling tolerances over short periods of time. But such stability alone is not a sufficient criterion for acceptance of the survey items, since it does not insure the validity of the concept as measured. Although survey items can often be compared to other objective records of the same characteristic or circumstance to test their validity (for example, occupation, age, income), when subjective evaluations are the subject of measurement no direct observations are possible. The respondents' stated beliefs must necessarily be accepted, as there is no recourse to external checks. And when the object of measurement is as multifaceted as interpersonal income evaluations, no single survey measure may adequately tap such a complex phenomenon. Analysis, therefore, must turn to indirect evidence consistent with theory and supported by demonstrated relationships to other observable variables.

Accordingly, before documenting differences among socioeconomic subgroups in their perceptions of income deprivation, analysis first explored the interrelationships among the several survey measures of deprivation, each tapping a different aspect of people's relative income position. By documenting these patterns of association, analysis illuminates the welfare implications of differences in the reported income evaluations among population subgroups.

In contrast to the test-retest reliability criteria, some real changes in people's perceptions of equity or deprivation can be reasonably expected to have occurred over the three-year period covered by the surveys, especially since this time period was nearly coincident with the 1974-75 recession. Price increases during the period were rapid, unemployment high, and increases in nominal wages were small—all important changes in the economic circumstances on which people base their sense of equity or deprivation.

Given this recessionary climate, what changes could we expect in estimates of the extent of wage or income deprivation? For example, since the November 1974 survey was taken about six months prior to the recession's low point, could we expect more people to voice income dissatisfaction at that time than might have been the case a year earlier or later? Did younger workers or those in blue-collar occupations voice greater wage deprivation as the recession increasingly constrained their opportunities?

Since these survey measurements were taken on independently drawn random cross-sectional samples, changes in the overall proportion reporting deprivation or equity do not necessarily imply similar changes among particular individuals. Moreover, even a stable reading on these survey measures does not preclude underlying individual change; whenever the proportion of respondents moving in the favorable direction equals the proportion changing in the unfavorable direction, the overall incidence of reported income deprivation or equity will remain unchanged.

Since income evaluations depend on both interpersonal and intertemporal (intrapersonal) comparisons, a declining economic environment may lead to less favorable intertemporal comparisons, but not necessarily to greater interpersonal deprivation. If economic adversity diminishes the fortunes of all uniformly, interpersonal comparisons may be left unaffected; on the other hand, a growing or stagnant economic environment, if accompanied by redistribution, may generate a great sense of interpersonal deprivation. In addition, aspirations for financial improvement, the implicit yardstick used to gauge satisfactions with current incomes, are also likely to be less pressing in times of adversity. Consequently, even though the 1974-75 recession was severe, it is unwarranted to expect its straightforward reflection in a greater sense of income deprivation.

Lastly, this chapter further elaborates on factors affecting income reference standards. As was noted in the previous chapter, the distributional standards that are advocated depend, in part, on economic circumstances as well as normative judgment. There is much evidence to suggest that reference standards are flexible and readily adjusted to changing economic circumstances.[1] Rainwater has found an extraordinary stability over an extended period of time in the amount of income people consider necessary to provide for comfortable living standards, and that people readily adjust this amount to current price levels.[2] In addition, the income and material aspirations people hold can also affect their income evaluations, since heightened aspirations diminish the importance of past accomplishments and increase the salience of continued income progress when making comparative evaluations. Providing the empirical documentation of these several links completes the foundation necessary for the full multivariate analysis model of the determinants of income evaluations.

SUBJECTIVE INCOME EVALUATIONS

Four separate items in each survey were used to assess different aspects of people's perceptions of equity or deprivation stemming from the current distribution of income. Two items focused on relative wage evaluations, and two asked respondents to rate their satisfaction with their own household income and material living standards.

Wage Comparisons

For wage comparisons, respondents were asked for separate evaluations based on intragroup and intergroup reference standards; one question asked respondents to compare their own income to what people received for doing the same type of work, another asked them to compare the income they received to how much people in other occupations earned. These items aimed at the overall subjective outcomes of evaluative comparisons by allowing respondents to use their own standards of fairness in making an assessment of what they felt they deserved in relation to both their own inputs and what other workers earn. The questions were worded as follows:

> How fair is what you earn on your job in *comparison to others* doing the same type of work you do? Do you feel that you get much less than you deserve, somewhat less than you deserve, about as much as you deserve, or more than you deserve in comparison with others in your line of work?

How fair is what people in your line of work earn *in comparison to how much people in other occupations earn*? Do you feel that you get much less than you deserve, somewhat less than you deserve, about as much as you deserve, or more than you deserve in comparison to how much people in *other* occupations earn?

Unfavorable comparisons of the latter type are often labeled fraternalistic deprivation, and those of the former as egoistic deprivation.[3] It is often maintained that fraternal, not egoistic, deprivation is most conducive to the perception of distributional inequity.[4] It is reasoned that egoistic deprivation has more to do with self-esteem, with the evaluation of one's personal circumstances in relation to what is attained by other group members. On the other hand, evaluations of income differences between occupational groups are taken to depend more on distributional preferences than on personal accomplishment. But a strict distinction is unwarranted as both evaluations are inherently rooted in one and the same income distribution. Although there may be less variance in income within occupations, these income differentials are no less subject to evaluations based on distributional preferences, nor are they without behavioral effect. In addition, since the extent of wage differentials within occupations also varies across different types of occupations, as the range of incomes among group members is widened, the likelihood is greater that distributional preferences will affect these comparative-wage evaluations. For example, among professional workers there may be greater within-group variance in income than at lower-skill levels. Furthermore, there may exist a tendency for people higher in socioeconomic status to be more individualistic in their viewpoint, more inclined to rely on their own personal progress in making comparative evaluations than on what relative gains are made by their group as a whole.[5]

Income Satisfaction

In addition to these wage evaluations, two more broadly based income valuations were elicited from respondents: satisfaction with family income and with their standard of living. Uisng a seven-point rating scale, respondents were asked: "How satisfied are you with the income you (and your family) have?" "How satisfied are you with your standard of living—the things you have like housing, car, furniture, recreation and the like?" These questions asked respondents to evaluate their share of economic rewards without regard to inputs or attribute differences, and leave the referents of comparison undefined. They are thus broader indicators of economic well-being or deprivation. Because consumption norms, somewhat apart from norms governing remuneration levels, are thought to be egalitarian,[6] these measured satisfactions were expected to demonstrate greater correspondence to notions of the reward levels themselves rather than the ratio of rewards to inputs.

TABLE 4.1

Subjective Income Evaluations of Working U.S. Adults, 1973-75 (percentages)

Evaluation	Comparison Within One's Own Occupation			Comparison Across Occupations		
	1973	1974	1975	1973	1974	1975
Earnings in comparison to other workers						
Much less (1)	15	14	11	21	16	17
Less (2)	28	26	27	32	34	32
Amount deserved (3)	53	57	57	41	46	45
More (5)	4	3	5	6	4	6
Total	100	100	100	100	100	100
Cases	762	835	749	754	820	747
	Total Family Income			**Standard of Living**		
	1973	1974	1975	1973	1974	1975
Extent of satisfaction with family income						
Dissatisfied (1-2)	9	12	7	7	4	3
Mostly satisfied (3)	11	13	10	7	5	5
Mixed Feelings (4)	20	21	18	18	13	15
Mostly satisfied (5)	37	31	36	40	38	34
Satisfied (6-7)	23	23	29	28	40	43
Total	100	100	100	100	100	100
Cases	802	864	776	802	861	778

Note: The base on which these percentage distributions were calculated excluded nonworking respondents and respondents for whom responses to these particular questions were not ascertained or where the respondents had stated that they "didn't know." In no instance did these excluded cases constitute more than 10 percent of eligible working respondents. In all subsequent analyses, this same practice of excluding cases with missing data on only those variables included in each particular analysis was followed.

Source: Survey Research Center, The University of Michigan.

Presented in Table 4.1 are the distributions of responses to each of the above four questions. As shown there, a majority of all respondents reported that they were satisfied with their family income and standard of living, and felt that their work income was equitable in comparison to others.

There were, however, important differences in the extent of reported income satisfaction and wage equity. Using the same rating scale, respondents voiced greater satisfaction with their standard of living than with their family income in each of the three surveys; and perceptions of wage equity were somewhat more widespread when respondents made comparisons with members of their own occupation than when they were asked to compare their wages across occupational lines. On average, more than seven in ten respondents rated themselves satisfied with their standard of living, whereas only six in ten, on average, rated themselves satisfied with their family income. In comparison, six in ten respondents, on average, said their wage income compared favorably to others in the same occupation, and just five in ten respondents rated their wage income favorably in comparison to those in other occupations.

These differences in income evaluations point to the difference between income adequacy and income equity; what was often found adequate, indeed reported as "satisfactory," was held as inequitably low by comparative standards. This distinction between income satisfaction and income equity was also observed at the individual level (see Table 4.4). Among respondents stating that they received "much less" than they deserve in comparison to other workers—whether within their own occupation or some other occupation—approximately one in three respondents also reported in each of the surveys that at the same time they were satisfied with their family income. Among those respondents who felt their wages in comparison to other workers were about what they deserve or greater, one in ten also reported income dissatisfaction.

The three successive yearly measurements of economic satisfaction and interpersonal wage comparisons did not indicate any significant overall trend (see Figure 4.2). As documented in the Appendix, changes over time in the responses to these items must exceed six percentage points, at minimum, in order to indicate significant differences (see Table A2). Although each question exhibited a somewhat characteristic distribution, as noted above, these distributions themselves showed little yearly change. Interestingly, although the reported level of income satisfaction declined somewhat in 1974, in that same year—near the low point in the recession—overall satisfaction with living standards improved somewhat. The marked contrast between the stability in subjective income evaluations and concurrent changes in the aggregate economy is highlighted in Table 4.2. Compared to the slight overall favorable drift in income evaluations, the prevailing trend in the aggregate economy was toward increasing prices and unemployment, and declines in output and in real income per household.

This absence of systematic aggregate change does not indicate the absence of change on the individual level, however. Many individuals may have changed in the favorable as well as the unfavorable direction, thus canceling in the aggregate. In addition, it should be carefully noted that changes in comparative income evaluations are dependent both on changes in actual income position and changes in the standards or criteria people apply. Income standards may rise with accomplishment, and therefore leave evaluations unchanged although real income improvements have been experienced. Similarly, income deterioration may also prompt more conservative income-reference standards, and hence lessen the sense of deprivation.

FIGURE 4.1

Trends in Wage and Income Evaluations, 1973-75

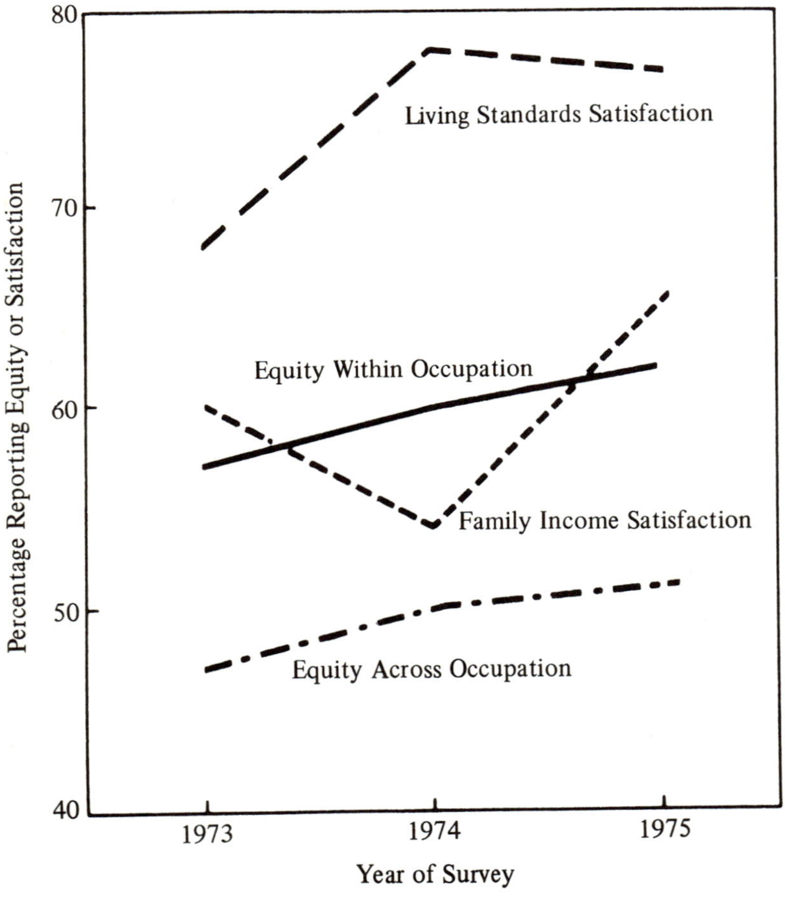

TABLE 4.2

Change in Aggregate Economic Conditions, 1973-75

Aggregate Condition	1973	1974	1975
Consumer prices[a]	6.4	11.0	9.1
Real income per household[a]	3.8	-1.2	-1.3
Real GNP[a]	5.5	-1.7	-1.8
Unemployment rate	4.9	5.6	8.5
Median household income[b]	$12,732	$12,220	$11,800

[a]Percentage change from prior year.
[b]Given in constant 1975 dollars.
Source: U.S. Department of Commerce, Bureau of the Census, and Bureau of Economic Analysis. Compiled by the author.

STRUCTURE OF INCOME EVALUATIONS

This stability of the aggregate incidence of reported equity or deprivation is further highlighted in Table 4.3, which reports the observed associations among these four income evaluations, and with the level of the respondent's earned income and their total family income. On average, the interitem association between the two wage comparison measures and between the two income satisfaction measures was substantial (The zero-order Pearson correlation was r = .42) and remained remarkably stable over the three survey measurements. Wage comparisons, on average, demonstrated a closer association with measured family income satisfaction (r = .29), than with reported satisfaction with living standards (r = .16). Although the association between wage comparisons and income satisfaction declined somewhat in the later surveys, these associations demonstrated great overall stability.

This stability also extended to the association between income evaluations and reported actual income levels. Although these subjective income evaluations demonstrated an important association with the income levels on which these evaluations were based (r = .20), the covariance was rather small. This suggests that perceptions of wage equity and income satisfaction are not simply dependent on actual income levels. Moreover, it should be noted that interpersonal wage comparisons, on average, demonstrated less of a correspondence to the respondent's actual income level (r = .14) than did the satisfaction measures (r = .23). This suggests that income differences are more often greeted with dissatisfaction than with a sense of inequity.

The significant and stable association between the two wage comparison measures (r = 0.41) indicates that these measures of sensed deprivation respond

TABLE 4.3

Associations among Subjective Income Evaluations and with Reported Income Levels

	1973				1974				1975			
Evaluation	(a)	(b)	(c)	(d)	(a)	(b)	(c)	(d)	(a)	(b)	(c)	(d)
(a) Wage comparisons within occupations	1.000	–	–	–	1.000	–	–	–	1.000	–	–	–
(b) Wage comparisons across occupations	.446	1.000	–	–	.399	1.000	–	–	.381	1.000	–	–
(c) Satisfaction with total family income	.357	.378	1.000	–	.304	.254	1.000	–	.231	.223	1.000	–
(d) Satisfaction with standard of living	.173	.174	.426	1.000	.164	.166	.464	1.000	.175	.113	.426	1.000
Respondent's income	.122	.147	.252	.176	.164	.101	.278	.218	.155	.168	.295	.176
Household's income	.125	.199	.295	.274	.118	.065	.313	.255	.125	.105	.341	.274

Note: For analysis purposes, respondents were scored according to the numbers within parentheses associated with the appropriate response category as detailed in Table 4.1; the number of cases included in each analysis are given in Table 4.1. Table entries are zero-order Pearson correlation coefficients.

to similar factors, beyond those specific to either within- or between-group comparisons. The size of this correlation in part reflects the delineation of the appropriate reference groups; the correlation between these two deprivation measures would approach unity if respondents used as referents only other occupational groups at or about their same relative economic status. In contrast, if each of the comparisons were made with reference to relatively distinct socioeconomic groups, the correspondence of these evaluative measures stemming from the overlapping reference groups can be expected to be at a minimum. Leon Festinger, John Thibaut and Harold Kelley, and George Homans have found that people tend to choose similar others as referents for a wide variety of comparisons. Accordingly, for example, the unskilled worker is unlikely to compare himself to a business executive when asked to make wage comparisons across occupations, but, rather, to skilled blue-collar workers. The data here also suggest that tendency.

Patterns of Association

This set of intercorrelations is suggestive of a patterning of these variables from the particular to the more general, from wage comparisons with stated occupational referents, to satisfaction with family income, and finally, to satisfaction with household living standards, the most inclusive measure of people's sense of economic well-being. In this sequence the current level of the respondent's earned income becomes an increasingly smaller portion of the economic rewards and resources on which these evaluations are based. Not only are multiple earners and other sources of additional income within households brought into consideration, but also accumulated wealth.

This line of reasoning is suggestive of the causal sequence as depicted in Figure 4.2, in the form of a path diagram, with the full regression statistics reported in Table 4.4. There we find that, as expected, wage comparisons affect voiced income satisfaction, which in turn has a significant effect on people's satisfaction with their material living standards. Furthermore, wage comparisons did not have any significant direct effect on satisfaction with living standards, their effect being completely mediated through the more general household income evaluations. A comparison of equations (2) through (4) in Table 4.4 provides clear evidence on this point: the (spurious) correlations between wage comparisons and satisfaction with living standards were reduced to zero when income satisfaction was also taken into account.

More Income Was Not Always More Satisfactory

Underlying this regression analysis was the familiar economic assumption that a greater income share is preferred to a smaller one, and, therefore, having

FIGURE 4.2

Pattern of Relationships among Measures of Subjective Income Evaluations

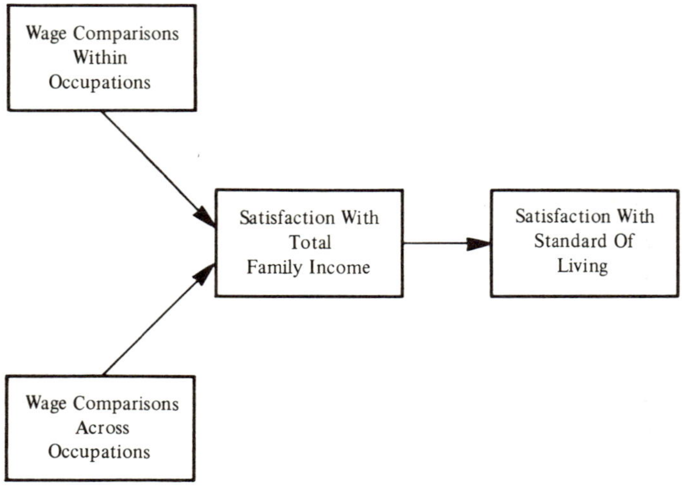

Note: The paths displayed were estimated to have significant standardized beta coefficients; the omitted paths–those between wage comparisons and satisfaction with living standards–failed to be empirically substantiated. See Table 4.4 for complete details on these regression analyses.

more will be judged more satisfactory than having less. Clearly, if people feel they are getting less pay than they deserve, they will also be less satisfied with their income. But does receiving more income mean people are also more satisfied, or does getting more pay than people feel they deserve only lessen income satisfaction? As was indicated in the previous chapter, after some point further increases in one's own income relative to others may only detract from, not add to, felt well-being. This feeling of declining welfare prompted by additions in one's own income was identified as occurring when incomes are in excess of normatively defined income reference standards (see Figures 3.2 and 3.3).

Table 4.5 reports the bivariate relationships between the two wage evaluations and satisfaction with income. There we find, as expected, that receiving less income than people felt they deserved was associated with a heightened sense of dissatisfaction. But the converse was not true: those who said they were getting more than they felt they deserved did not report greater satisfaction than those who felt that they were being paid equitably. Receiving more was not held more satisfactory than being paid a fair amount; yet, at the same time, it was

TABLE 4.4

Regression Analysis of Subjective Income Evaluations, 1973-75

Independent Variable	1973				1974				1975			
	Satisfaction with Total Family Income	Satisfaction with Standard of Living			Satisfaction with Total Family Income	Satisfaction with Standard of Living			Satisfaction with Total Family Income	Satisfaction with Standard of Living		
	(1)	(2)	(3)	(4)	(1)	(2)	(3)	(4)	(1)	(2)	(3)	(4)
Wage comparisons within occupations	.235 (6.38)	–	.119 (2.96)	.021 (0.55)	.242 (6.69)	–	.117 (3.10)	.008 (0.23)	.170 (4.45)	–	.155 (3.95)	.085 (2.34)
Wage comparisons across occupations	.274 (7.43)	–	.122 (3.04)	.008 (0.20)	.157 (4.36)	–	.120 (3.18)	.049 (1.42)	.157 (4.11)	–	.054 (1.37)	-.011 (0.30)
Satisfaction with total family income	–	.426 (12.88)		.416 (11.32)	–	.464 (14.88)	–	.449 (13.57)	–	.426 (12.79)	–	.409 (11.84)
Constant	2.84	2.97	4.04	2.92	2.70	3.51	4.35	3.38	3.49	3.48	4.52	3.30
See	1.18	1.12	1.22	1.12	1.37	1.04	1.15	1.04	1.26	1.02	1.11	1.02
RSQD (adjusted)	.185	1.81	.139	.179	.111	.214	.037	.215	.072	.180	.031	.085

Note: The wage comparison variables were scored as follows: much less (1), less (2), same (3), and more (5). The satisfaction variables were scaled as detailed in Table 4.1. Table entries are standardized beta coefficients with associated t-statistics in parentheses. For the number of cases, see Table 4.1.

TABLE 4.5

Bivariate Relationship between Wage Comparisons and Income Satisfaction

	Income Satisfaction (percent of respondents)						
	Dissatisfied	Mixed	Satisfied				
Wage Comparison	(1-3)	(4)	(5-7)	Total	Mean Satisfaction Score		Cases
			1973				
Within occupations							
Much less	45	21	34	100	3.72		113
Less	25	31	44	100	4.14		211
About what respondent deserves	10	15	75	100	4.97	*	404
More	9	16	75	100	5.13		32
Across occupations							
Much less	46	20	34	100	3.65		155
Less	20	29	51	100	4.40	*	240
About what respondent deserves	8	15	77	100	5.04		311
More	11	15	74	100	5.15		46
			1974				
Within occupations							
Much less	49	21	30	100	3.46		117
Less	31	25	44	100	4.07	*	217
About what respondent deserves	17	20	63	100	4.67		467
More	8	15	77	100	5.12		26
Across occupations							
Much less	46	21	33	100	3.61		132
Less	25	29	46	100	4.19	*	271
About what respondent deserves	18	17	65	100	4.73		377
More	18	9	73	100	4.70		33
			1975				
Within occupations							
Much less	38	17	45	100	3.93		84
Less	19	25	56	100	4.46	*	200
About what respondent deserves	13	16	71	100	4.91		427
More	18	3	79	100	5.00		34
Across occupations							
Much less	31	16	53	100	4.28		127
Less	20	26	54	100	4.48		239
About what respondent deserves	12	14	74	100	4.91	*	337
More	10	3	87	100	5.35		40

*T-tests indicate these paired means are significantly different from one another at the .05 level.

considered much more satisfactory than receiving less than you felt you deserved. This pattern of responses suggests that in scaling the responses to wage comparisons in terms of satisfaction, the condition of wage equity would receive the highest satisfaction score (5); receiving more than you feel you deserve is somewhat less satisfactory and therefore would get a lower score (4), but higher than the score given respondents who said they received less (2) or much less (1) pay than they deserved. In contrast, in the abovementioned regression equations (see Table 4.4), the wage comparison variables were scaled from more pay (5) to much less (1), with the condition of equity receiving an intermediate score (3). To investigate this difference in scaling, the above regression analysis was replicated, after the wage comparison variables were rescaled according to the above scheme (see Table 4.6).

A comparison of the two sets of regressions reveals almost identical results: the rescaled wage variables account for about the same amount of variance in income satisfaction, and wage comparisons still show no direct impact on the more general satisfaction with living standards. Thus these data are at least consistent with the view that less income may be preferred to more when having more would have otherwise made an inequitably high income higher, even if this means your own income must now undergo relative decline.

SUBGROUP DIFFERENCES IN INCOME EVALUATIONS

An important element in understanding the welfare content of these evaluations is the comparative incidence of favorable and unfavorable evaluation among various population subgroups, and any evidence that might indicate potential trends in shifting income evaluations among these subgroups. Presented in Tables 4.7-4.10 are the breakdowns of income evaluations within various demographic classifications for the three surveys. As a guide for estimating the significance of differences in the reported percentages—between subgroups both within the same survey and across the three independent samples—approximate measurement errors are presented in the appendix (see Tables A1-A2).

Income Position

The breakdown of wage evaluations across income classes again indicates that people's sense of equity was dependent on more than just relative income position. There were no systematic differences in evaluations among those with earned incomes of less than $15,000. Only above an earned income level of $15,000 was there a substantial shift toward felt wage equity, but even among these high-income workers one in four still reported a sense of wage deprivation.

A similar weak association between subjective income satisfaction and reported income levels was also evidenced. Although there was a greater overall

TABLE 4.6

Regression Analysis of Subjective Income Evaluations Adjusted for Potential Nonlinear Response Patterns

Independent Variable	1973 Satisfaction with Total Family Income	1973 Satisfaction with Standard of Living			1974 Satisfaction with Total Family Income	1974 Satisfaction with Standard of Living			1975 Satisfaction with Total Family Income	1975 Satisfaction with Standard of Living		
	(1)	(2)	(3)	(4)	(1)	(2)	(3)	(4)	(1)	(2)	(3)	(4)
Wage comparisons within occupations	.250[b] (6.64)	–	.140 (3.40	.036 (0.94)	.217 (5.88)	–	.147 (3.82)	.049 (1.39)	.188 (4.73)	–	.132 (3.22)	.052 (1.38)
Wage comparisons across occupations	.270 (7.19)	–	.107 (2.61)	-.005 (0.12)	.177 (4.79)	–	.075 (1.96)	-.004 (.116)	.119 (2.99)	–	.014 (0.35)	-.036 (0.95)
Satisfaction with total family income	–	.426 (12.88)		.414 (10.90)	–	.464 (14.88)		.450 (13.62)	–	.426 (12.79)	–	.421 (12.18)
Constant	3.20	.297	4.19	2.94	3.15	3.51	4.58	3.44	3.81	3.48	4.82	3.45
See	1.17	1.12	1.21	1.12	1.37	1.04	1.15	1.04	1.27	1.02	1.12	1.02
RSQD (adjusted)	.200	.181	.179	.110	.214	.035	.214	.067	.067	.180	.017	.180

Note: For this analysis only the wage-comparison variables were scored as follows: much less (1), less (2), more (4), and same (5). Table entries are standardized beta coefficients with associated t-statistics in parentheses.

correspondence between income level and income satisfaction, the largest shift toward reported satisfaction came only when reported income levels reached $15,000 or more.

Over the three-year period covered by these surveys, no income class showed significant trends toward either improvement or deterioration in their self-reported income evaluations.

In addition to income, other demographic classifications have often been used to trace the effects of income distribution on people's sense of equity. Women and racial minorities, for example, have often been isolated as subgroups that have suffered disproportionately from inequitably low wages. As shown in Tables 4.7–4.10, nonwhite respondents were not only more likely to report they received less pay than they deserved, but they also reported greater dissatisfaction with their overall economic situation. By margins of approximately ten percentage points, nonwhite respondents more frequently voiced wage deprivation. And these racial differences were even larger for reported satisfaction with income and standard of living. On average, four in ten nonwhite respondents reported themselves dissatisfied with their family income, as compared to just two in ten white respondents. Reported satisfaction with living standard was 30 percentage points higher among white respondents.

Among white respondents, females did not report a greater sense of wage deprivation, either within or across occupations. Since it has been widely documented that women, on average, receive less work income than similarly qualified men, a greater sense of wage deprivation was expected. This lack of correspondence to perceptions of income equity may suggest that either comparisons were made largely to occupational referents of the same sex, or that women, on average, perceived their inputs to be correspondingly less and so brought their evaluations into line with the lower incomes they actually receive.

Socioeconomic Characteristics

When respondents were classified according to their own occupation, income comparisons made within people's own occupation showed no discernible pattern. Managers and business officials, however—those most likely to use income differentials as evaluative criteria for gauging their own career prospects—reported somewhat less deprivation in each of the three surveys. For them, it may not only be that they are likely to make more informed comparisons, but also that their self-esteem is tied more to the outcome of this type of evaluative comparison; they are consequently more apt to view their circumstance in a favorable light. When evaluations were made across occupations, unskilled blue-collar workers reported more fraternalistic deprivation than skilled blue-collar workers. This result plausibly reflects the fact that the average earnings for members of these occupational groups are not only among the lowest, but are also

TABLE 4.7

Reported Wage Equity within Workers' Own Occupations, among Major Population Subgroups, 1973-75

	1973				1974				1975			
Subgroup	Amount Deserved or More	Somewhat Less	Much Less	Cases	Amount Deserved or More	Somewhat Less	Much Less	Cases	Amount Deserved or More	Somewhat Less	Much Less	Cases
All respondents	57%	28%	15%	762	60%	26%	14%	844	62%	27%	11%	749
Sex/race												
Male/white	59	29	12	415	62	26	12	418	63	28	9	411
Male/non-white	37	46	17	46	55	24	21	66	51	22	27	45
Female/white	63	22	15	256	62	24	14	288	63	26	11	250
Female/non-white	31	33	36	45	46	35	19	72	51	27	22	45
Occupation												
Professional/technical	56	31	13	134	57	27	16	128	67	24	9	138
Managers and officials	68	22	10	94	65	23	12	136	67	25	8	93
Clerical and sales	60	27	13	156	59	31	10	185	63	26	11	158
Craftsmen and foremen	51	34	15	131	59	27	14	117	51	33	16	120
Operatives	58	21	21	127	53	25	22	122	65	21	14	114
Laborers/service	49	32	19	93	63	25	12	129	59	29	12	114

Income												
Less than $5,000	55	26	19	226	57	30	13	244	48	35	17	161
$5,000-7,499	52	31	17	124	49	24	27	116	63	29	8	106
$7,500-9,999	51	32	17	119	61	24	15	123	66	21	13	113
$10,000-12,499	52	30	18	88	60	28	12	115	64	24	12	95
$12,500-14,999	59	34	7	61	57	32	11	73	67	20	13	79
$15,000 or more	74	22	4	96	73	21	6	137	67	28	5	142
Age												
18-24	61	27	12	148	55	30	15	146	52	32	16	109
25-34	56	25	19	197	58	25	17	244	61	26	13	237
35-44	60	28	12	147	65	24	11	169	63	25	12	167
45-54	59	26	15	148	56	30	14	161	69	26	5	123
55-64	51	36	13	97	67	20	13	108	62	30	8	95
Education												
9-11 grades or less	51	29	20	206	55	30	15	177	56	31	13	179
High school	63	23	14	301	60	28	12	305	63	25	12	282
Some college	57	34	9	126	63	20	17	193	59	31	10	143
College or advanced degree	56	30	14	126	63	24	13	164	66	24	10	147

Note: See Tables A1-A2 for the percentage differences required for significance.

TABLE 4.8

Reported Wage Equity across Occupations, among Major Population Subgroups, 1973-75

Subgroup	1973				1974				1975			
	Amount Deserved or More	Somewhat Less	Much Less	Cases	Amount Deserved or More	Somewhat Less	Much Less	Cases	Amount Deserved or More	Somewhat Less	Much Less	Cases
All respondents	47%	32%	21%	754	51%	33%	16%	829	51%	32%	17%	747
Sex/race												
Male/white	50	33	17	411	54	32	14	418	54	31	15	413
Male/non-white	41	46	13	46	52	27	21	63	40	28	32	43
Female/white	48	27	25	256	48	33	19	276	48	35	17	251
Female/non-white	19	39	42	41	39	43	18	72	43	33	24	42
Occupation												
Professional/technical	44	39	17	135	41	35	24	127	43	39	18	136
Managers and officials	53	33	14	92	61	31	8	135	66	25	9	94
Clerical and sales	55	28	17	151	53	31	16	182	55	30	15	159
Craftsmen and foremen	50	31	19	131	57	31	12	113	51	33	16	118
Operatives	44	28	28	126	46	34	20	123	50	35	15	111
Laborers/service	39	31	30	93	45	38	17	123	42	30	28	117

Income												
Less than $5,000	43	29	28	221	43	38	19	237	34	39	27	160
$5,000-7,499	46	30	24	123	45	31	24	114	48	36	16	106
$7,500-9,999	43	37	20	118	54	32	14	123	54	32	14	111
$10,000-12,499	51	34	15	88	44	40	16	114	58	22	20	94
$12,500-14,999	41	39	20	61	59	28	13	76	49	37	14	78
$15,000 or more	66	28	6	96	62	27	11	135	61	29	10	142
Age												
18-24	50	35	15	143	52	30	18	141	39	45	16	109
25-34	50	30	20	192	53	33	14	237	51	30	19	235
35-44	47	33	20	146	52	32	16	167	53	31	16	167
45-54	48	30	22	152	46	34	20	158	57	30	13	122
55-64	42	34	24	94	49	37	14	110	52	29	19	97
Education												
9-11 grades or less	45	27	28	205	43	40	17	172	52	30	18	175
High school	51	31	18	294	53	33	14	305	53	31	16	282
Some college	49	36	15	129	53	30	17	186	51	31	18	144
College or advanced degree	41	41	18	124	48	31	21	162	43	39	18	147

Note: See Tables A1-A2 for the percentage differences required for significance.

TABLE 4.9

Reported Satisfaction with Family Income, among Major Population Subgroups, 1973-75

	1973				1974				1975			
Subgroup	Satisfied	Mixed	Dissatisfied	Cases	Satisfied	Mixed	Dissatisfied	Cases	Satisfied	Mixed	Dissatisfied	Cases
All respondents	60%	20%	20%	802	53%	21%	26%	864	64%	18%	18%	776
Sex/race												
Male/white	66	18	16	431	59	21	20	437	71	15	14	424
Male/nonwhite	30	30	40	47	48	14	38	63	46	24	30	46
Female/white	61	22	17	269	49	26	25	292	61	22	17	262
Female/nonwhite	31	27	42	55	44	13	43	72	34	21	45	44
Occupation												
Professional/technical	64	19	17	140	63	20	17	135	72	19	9	141
Managers and officials	72	17	11	102	65	21	14	148	76	16	8	98
Clerical and sales	61	21	18	165	50	24	26	187	58	19	23	165
Craftsmen and foremen	58	22	20	133	57	22	21	119	68	18	14	124
Operatives	58	19	23	135	52	17	31	122	58	15	27	116
Laborers/service	41	28	31	101	35	24	41	128	58	22	20	118

Income												
Less than $5,000	49	25	26	237	46	20	34	242	51	19	30	116
$5,000-7,499	52	22	26	132	35	25	40	118	53	22	25	110
$7,500-9,999	61	18	21	126	53	22	25	124	60	21	19	113
$10,000-12,499	60	26	14	90	56	27	17	119	65	20	15	96
$12,500-14,999	66	16	18	62	64	20	16	80	75	15	10	81
$15,000 or more	84	12	4	100	75	15	10	144	82	13	5	147
Age												
18-24	54	25	21	151	50	22	28	144	57	21	22	107
25-34	54	24	22	205	49	25	26	251	61	20	19	247
35-44	65	18	17	154	60	16	24	167	65	18	17	174
45-54	64	16	20	161	51	24	25	171	65	19	16	127
55-64	70	18	12	103	60	21	19	113	76	10	14	100
Education												
9-11 grades or less	51	21	28	219	46	18	36	176	62	17	21	185
High school	66	17	17	317	55	22	23	314	65	17	18	291
Some college	54	29	17	133	54	24	22	179	65	19	16	145
College or advanced degree	65	20	15	134	55	29	26	139	69	18	13	154

Note: See Tables A1-A2 for the percentage differences required for significance.

TABLE 4.10

Reported Satisfaction with Living Standards, among Major Population Subgroups, 1973-75

	1973				1974				1975			
Subgroup	Satisfied	Mixed	Dissatisfied	Cases	Satisfied	Mixed	Dissatisfied	Cases	Satisfied	Mixed	Dissatisfied	Cases
All respondents	69%	17%	14%	802	78%	13%	9%	861	78%	15%	7%	778
Sex/race												
Male/white	71	20	9	430	81	11	8	436	81	14	5	424
Male/nonwhite	46	15	39	48	77	6	17	61	60	19	21	47
Female/white	74	14	12	269	79	12	9	294	78	17	5	262
Female/nonwhite	49	20	31	55	59	15	26	70	60	11	30	45
Occupation												
Professional/technical	73	16	11	140	86	10	4	135	81	13	6	141
Managers and officials	79	11	10	102	81	14	5	145	90	9	1	98
Clerical and sales	68	20	12	165	76	13	11	185	75	17	8	167
Craftsmen and fore-men	65	24	11	133	82	11	7	120	76	21	3	125
Operatives	68	14	18	136	76	13	11	123	76	14	10	116
Laborers/service	57	21	22	100	70	14	16	127	73	11	16	117

Income												
Less than $5,000	63	17	20	237	71	14	15	243	73	16	11	166
$5,000-7,499	67	16	17	131	67	16	17	116	72	18	10	110
$7,500-9,999	69	22	9	126	84	11	5	123	73	19	8	113
$10,000-12,499	67	25	8	90	80	12	8	119	76	16	8	97
$12,500-14,999	74	11	15	62	85	11	4	80	83	12	5	81
$15,000 or more	85	15	–*	100	92	7	1	144	88	10	2	147
Age												
18-24	66	21	13	150	70	19	11	142	74	13	13	110
25-34	65	19	16	205	75	13	12	248	72	20	8	246
35-44	72	16	12	155	83	12	5	169	80	12	8	173
45-54	71	16	13	161	83	10	7	172	83	14	3	128
55-64	70	15	15	103	82	10	8	112	82	12	6	100
Education												
9-11 grades or less	64	19	17	219	73	14	13	177	76	12	12	186
High school	71	16	13	315	79	11	10	314	78	13	9	291
Some college	65	22	13	133	74	19	7	177	77	15	8	146
College or advanced degree	72	21	7	132	86	7	7	137	77	20	3	154

*Indicates less than 0.5 percent.

Note: See Tables A1-A2 for the percentage differences required for significance.

low relative to other blue-collar workers, their likely referents when making wage comparisons. Interestingly, members of the professional and technical occupations were consistently less favorable, in each of the three surveys, in their income evaluations across occupational groups. Although respondents with professional occupations were among the best paid, they were similar to the unskilled blue-collar worker in this evaluation.

In all, classification by occupation did not yield strong relationships to sensed deprivation, either for within- or between-group comparisons. This result was not unexpected. Comparisons of the ratio of rewards to inputs should not be affected by what occupational group people are members of, when comparisons are made within this group. For between-group comparisons, an occupation-deprivation relationship results only when one group is underpaid for its inputs in relation to other groups. While systematic underevaluation of labor inputs may well exist, it is not usually confined to skills needed in particular occupations; rather, it is most often associated with ascriptive factors such as race and sex.

Young workers, those most likely to have lower absolute incomes, voiced no more deprivation than did their older colleagues. This suggests that if age did not represent a relevant input—experience—of which they supplied less, younger workers would voice more deprivation, not less. It is also of interest to note that education was not systematically related to sensed deprivation. Although differences in age and education were not directly related to felt deprivation, the analysis contained in the next chapter demonstrated that these variables have a significant indirect effect on comparative evaluations. It was found that the standards applied for judging the equitability of income differences did take into account differences in age, education, and work experience.

In contrast with the absence of a direct relationship between age and wage equity, there was a more systematic association between income and reports of income and standard-of-living satisfaction. This results in part from the accumulated increases in income and assets that are associated with the advancing age of the household. In addition, since satisfaction is hypothesized to depend on the level of aspirations as well as the current level of income, advancing years may not only add to accumulated material holdings, but may also lessen material aspirations. This effect of age on aspirations has been documented elsewhere.[7]

SUMMARY

The results of this chapter can be summarized as follows. First, the majority of all working Americans reported favorable income evaluations during the entire 1973-75 period. Although barely 50 percent of all workers in each year studied felt equitably treated in comparison to what workers in other occupations earn, a more substantial majority of three in four reported themselves satisfied with their standard of living. Overall, people's sense of deprivation stemming from unfavorable wage comparisons was more extensive than dissatisfaction with family income or living standards. Of the two wage comparisons, more respondents reported wage equity within their own occupation than in comparison to other occupations; and satisfaction with living standards was more frequently voiced than with family income levels.

In addition, the overall proportion of respondents who reported either a sense of income equity or satisfaction was remarkably stable over the three-year period in which these surveys were taken. In part, the stability in perceptions of equity or deprivation represents the stability of the income distribution itself, although many individuals may have changed in a favorable or unfavorable direction during this period. Because increases in consumer prices during much of this period exceeded nominal income increases, the stability of these voiced income evaluations also indicates that the criteria on which these evaluations were based shifted along with changing economic circumstances.

An examination of the interrelationships among these income evaluations themselves revealed an underlying structure to subjective income evaluations, whereby wage comparisons fed into income satisfaction, which in turn affected satisfaction with overall household living standards. Importantly, wage comparisons had no direct impact on satisfaction with living standards. The same structure of evaluations was replicated in all three surveys. These results suggest that perceptions of interpersonal-wage inequity had only a limited and indirect impact on more basic economic satisfaction, their influence being filtered by satisfaction with income levels. This implies that a sense of wage inequity can only be expected to be translated into a more general type of economic dissatisfaction or alienation when income levels are seen as unsatisfactorily low as well as inequitable.

Another important facet of the structure of income evaluations revealed that overpayment—receiving more pay than the worker thought he deserved in comparison to others—was not associated with greater economic well-being. In each survey, the data indicated that more income was not always found more satisfactory. This finding is important because it indicates that people's distributional preferences, which underpin these income evaluations, do not necessarily associate greater individual well-being with a greater share of individual income.

Demographic profiles of income evaluations only revealed small overall differences among the major population subgroups, and that these differences held largely intact during the entire period analyzed. Importantly, relative socioeconomic position demonstrated only a small impact on people's income evaluations. Rather than finding differences in economic experience leading to polarized or steeply divergent subjective income evaluations, U.S. workers voiced a widespread and enduring sense of income equity and satisfaction.

NOTES

1. George Katona, *Psychological Economics* (New York: Elsevier, 1975).

2. Lee Rainwater, *What Money Buys: Inequality and the Social Meanings of Income* (New York: Basic Books, 1974).

3. James A. Davis, "A Formal Interpretation of the Theory of Relative Deprivation," *Sociometry* 22 (December 1959): 280-96; Walter G. Runciman, *Relative Deprivation and Social Justice* (Berkeley: University of California Press, 1966), and Ted R. Gurr, *Why Men Rebel*, (Princeton: Princeton University Press, 1970).

4. See, for example, Reeve D. Vanneman and Thomas F. Pettigrew, "Race and Relative Deprivation in the Urban United States," *Race* 13 (April 1972): 461-86.

5. Runciman, op. cit. See also Paul S. Goodman, "An Examination of Referents Used in the Evaluation of Pay," *Organizational Behavior and Human Performance* 12 (October 1974): 170-95; Goodman provides empirical support for his hypothesis that "the greater the level of professionalism, the greater the selection of referents outside the focal organization."

6. Phillip Brickman and Donald T. Campbell, "Hedonic Relativism and Planning the Good Society," in *Adaptation Level Theory: A Symposium*, ed. M. H. Appley (New York: Academic Press, 1972).

7. Gunter Schmolders, and Bernd Biervert, "Level of Aspiration and Consumption Standard: Some General Findings," in *Human Behavior in Economic Affairs*, ed. Burkhard Strumpel, James N. Morgan, and Ernest Zahn (New York: Elsevier Scientific Publishing Co., 1972), pp. 213-27.

CHAPTER

5

BASES OF INTERPERSONAL COMPARISONS

On what do people base their perceptions of income equity or claims of deprivation? It is important to determine what factors affect these judgments because they tell us how people translate their relative economic position into a personal sense of well-being. In this chapter, empirical estimates based on the objective counterparts of people's perceptions of relative deprivation or gratification are detailed and analyzed.

To establish the framework for this empirical investigation, the underlying interpersonal comparison model must be more thoroughly delineated and carefully scrutinized. Several aspects of interpersonal income comparisons are of particular concern. First, the normative income standard or distributional criterion that is used determines the form of comparison. If equal shares are advocated as the appropriate income standard, not only are differences in inputs discounted when making interpersonal comparisons, but the rewards on which these comparisons are based are also likely to be more broadly defined—including not only what income people earn themselves, but all incomes and other economic resources available to their household. Alternatively, if an input proportionality criterion is advocated, how much people earn themselves is clearly the appropriate reward basis for comparisons. Less clear is which inputs should count and by how much when assessing interpersonal income differentials.

This chapter reports on a detailed analysis of these issues. The 1973 survey directly questioned respondents as to the appropriateness of various criteria for determining wage equity. These data indicated a preference for performance related criteria when judging the fairness of wage differentials. In addition, adherence to this productivity standard was widespread and held strong appeal across all socioeconomic subgroups. Several empirical estimates of income deprivation—

based on reported income levels adjusted for potential differences in evaluative standards—were then introduced and contrasted. In one version, differences in income levels and wage changes were compared to the reported average received among all workers in that year. In another, a human capital model was utilized to simulate differences in productive inputs as compared to differences in wage incomes.

Lastly, this chapter further elaborates on factors affecting income referent choice. As noted in the previous chapters, which distributional standards are advocated depend on economic circumstance as well as normative judgment. Aspirations for real income gain and people's opinions on how inflation has affected their own relative income position were singled out for further investigation. Providing the conceptual foundation of these several links completes the foundation necessary for the full multivariate analysis model of the determinants of income evaluations, which is the subject of the following chapter.

RELATIVE ECONOMIC STATUS

Equal Share Criterion

For comparisons made under an equalitarian norm of reward distribution, an individual's level of earned income (or its change) can be compared to the societal average, an amount which would be attainable if everyone shared equally. Using the sample mean as an income reference standard, empirical estimates would simply take the form,

$$Y_i \lesseqgtr \overline{Y}\ ;$$

$$\%\,\Delta\, Y_i \lesseqgtr \overline{\%\,\Delta\, Y}.$$

All respondents with reported income (or change) of less than the sample average would be considered relatively deprived under these estimates.*

A more comprehensive measure of relative economic status based on egalitarian standards would also include allowances for household composition and

---

*The survey questions were as follows: "To get an accurate picture of people's financial situation, we need to know the income of all people we interview. How much did you earn from your job in . . . (year prior to survey), before taxes and other deductions were made?" And, "How large was your last pay increase, either from a raise or job change?" For analysis, percentage increases were first rank ordered and then partitioned into five groups of equal size, and scored one to five accordingly. Such data transformations were required because of the extent of intermediate-data manipulation needed to generate percentage figures from responses given in dollar amounts.

need. Concern with the maintenance of minimum living standards in society goes back to ancient times. At first this concern was identified with charity; now, in the age of mass affluence amidst widespread poverty, much of this concern has shifted to the general problem of income distribution. Accordingly, attention has shifted from subsistence-level budgets to adequate living levels, and finally to comfortable living levels.[1] To capture the basic dimensions of family income adequacy, the following measure was computed and designated welfare ratio (WR) since it expressed the relation of household needs to its means:

$$WR = \frac{\text{total family income}}{\$1{,}600 + \$800\,(\text{family size})}$$

This ratio attains a value of WR = 1 for a family of four with a household income of $4,800, which was approximately the officially defined poverty level during the time these data were collected. Estimates of relative deprivation based on this measure take the form,

$$WR_i \lesseqgtr \overline{WR},$$

the average welfare ratio serving as the standard of comparison. Consequently, not only the so-called officially poor, but all people whose households fall below average material living standards, were taken to be relatively deprived under this standard of distribution.

These empirical estimates reflect two important facets of an equal share criterion for reward distribution: equality of rewards by definition establishes a single societal reference standard that is used by everyone in making comparisons; and, given that everyone should be treated equally regardless of inputs, issues concerning which inputs should count in determining pay rates, and how much they should count, are avoided. In contrast, estimates of deprivation based on a distributional rule, which holds that rewards should be in proportion to inputs, are less straightforward. Analysis not only needs to specify which inputs are relevant for comparative income evaluations, but also needs to simultaneously determine the terms of exchange of inputs into rewards in order to estimate the appropriate income reference standard used by individuals in making interpersonal comparisons.

Proportional Share Criterion

Economic theory gives ample guidance for the selection of input variables on which to base a proportional share criterion. The relation of factor rewards to market conditions and productivity differentials has been widely researched and documented.[2] Indeed, marginal productivity theory has long been held a cornerstone of the so-called neo-classical theory of income distribution.[3] Milton Friedman, and Franco Modigliani and Richard Brumberg further expanded our understanding of the dynamic interplay of these factors over time by the notion of permanent or life-cycle patterns of income and consumption.[4] And James Duesenberry, in explicating the social character of consumption patterns, outlined a framework in which reference standards play a central role in economic choice.[5] According to this line of reasoning, people come to expect different profiles of income over their working life cycles—wage contours—for different combinations of inputs. These income expectations represent more than just expected command over material resources. They also represent a standard by which people may evaluate themselves in relation to others, and thus learn about themselves through a process of social comparisons.[6]

Empirical estimates of comparisons between one's own and referent income made under a proportional rule of distribution were derived by first taking the mean income for all those having the same input characteristics as an income reference standard. The magnitude of discrepancy between current work income and input-reference standard was then estimated as follows:

$$ID_i = Y_i - \hat{Y} \tag{5.1}$$

$$\hat{Y}_i = \bar{Y} + \sum_{x=1}^{n} a_{ix} \tag{5.2}$$

where Y_i is annual work income.* The a_{ix} adjustments to the overall mean income represent the effects of the contribution of each input on the individual's income reference standard. When ID_i is positive, a favorable comparison is implied; when there exists a negative discrepancy, relative deprivation is indicated. Thus, this measure of deprivation was responsive to differences in income for given input characteristics; this may be termed individualistic deprivation (ID).

Group deprivation (GD) was estimated as follows:

$$GD_i = Y_i - \bar{Y}. \tag{5.3}$$

When this quantity was positive, the expected income for those with these same input characteristics exceeded the overall average income level and pointed toward a favorable relative income position for this input reference. When negative, group deprivation was indicated insofar as the input reference standard compares unfavorably to the overall mean income. More generally, relative expected incomes can be interpreted as representing differences in permanent incomes.[7] It would thus follow that deviations of expected from mean income mirror what are rather stable differentials of relative group incomes. This measure of deprivation was then more responsive to structural and institutional factors, as reflected by group differentials, than to interindividual variations in income.

---

*Other formulations were tried, including the raio of expected to mean income, but to no avail.

These two measures combined represent the total deviation of observed income around its sample mean:

$$DI_i + DF_i = (Y_i - \hat{Y}_i) + (\hat{Y}_i - \bar{Y}) = Y_i - \bar{Y}. \qquad (5.4)$$

By summing these parts, this total also represented the magnitude of income discrepancy as calculated from a strict equalitarian rule of reward distribution. Here relative deprivation simply becomes the semantic inverse of relative income, as overall mean income is taken as the universal standard of comparison, as was the case under the equal-share criterion.

It should be noted that the discrepancy between one's own income and the mean income of those having the same input characteristics has a very large residual, and there is no good reason to suppose that this residual is truly random. For example, suppose that an income equation is able to explain 40 percent of the variance of observed annual earnings. This means that 60 percent of the variation in income is not explicable in terms of the set of input factors used, and of that residual variance, part is truly random with respect to inputs, but part is a reflection of inputs that were not measured. Any inputs that were not measured and form part of the individual's own set of input reference standards will produce a bias in these estimates. Moreover, suppose, for example, that people with higher incomes than predicted are also people who place a higher value on leisure than on money income, or on intrinsic work rewards than on monetary compensation. People do not necessarily sense relative deprivation just because they earn less money than expected; other factors may also enter into their evaluations.

On the other hand, the estimate of group deprivation may not have quite the same extent of bias as the measure of individual deprivation, since some of the unmeasured influences on an individual basis will tend to wash out at the group level. Not all of this bias, however, can be expected to cancel out, since, for example, some occupations may tend to attract people who contribute relatively large amounts of unmeasured (or interpersonally unmeasurable) inputs, while others attract people who contribute significantly lesser amounts of unmeasured inputs (for example, artists as opposed to craftsmen).

It is a more systematic investigation of input criteria that analysis now turns.

BASES OF COMPARISON

What inputs or individual characteristics form the basis of comparisons? Ability, skills, experience, seniority, and the amount of work time are most often utilized in assessing income differences. These factors provide a basis for interpersonal income evaluations. Factors such as race and sex, however, while they relate to actual income differences, may not be accepted as appropriate inputs on which the distribution of income ought to be based. The decision to include or disallow such factors depends on how people take account of such differences in making welfare comparisons, on how normative standards affect their choice of referent, not on whether market rewards actually accrue to these input characteristics. Male-female income differences are, in part, at issue here. Are evaluative comparisons restricted to the incomes of same-sexed referents with similar skills and abilities, even though women often earn less than men in similar jobs? The preliminary readings of people's perceptions of income equity detailed in the last chapter suggest that women do not sense relative deprivation, nor men gratification, stemming from the existing income differentials between the sexes.

Furthermore, differences in evaluative comparisons may also result from the extent to which people think the various input factors should count. For example, income differentials that are accorded experienced workers may be considered excessive, even though some pay differentials may be considered appropriate.* Moreover, less consensus can be expected on this issue since people's perceptions of the amounts of inputs supplied by others may well differ, and differ widely, whereas social norms, on which agreement is more widespread, largely govern which inputs are selected as appropriate bases for comparison.

Preferred Wage Criteria

What inputs do U.S. workers consider relevant? Working respondents in the fall 1973 survey were asked the following questions:

> People have different ideas about what should count in deciding what amount of pay is fair. People feel some things should count more than they do now. Other things should count less. I'd like to ask you about your ideas.

---

*Furthermore, changes in evaluative criteria may occasion widespread shifts in welfare comparisons, and these changes may be concentrated among particular population subgroups. For example, the elimination of seniority as an evaluative criterion would make the relatively lower wages of younger workers less acceptable. If the elimination of seniority were gradual, proceeding from young to old, unfavorable welfare comparisons would be concentrated among the young with no offsetting effects generated from comparisons made by older workers. Similarly, changes in evaluative criteria based on sex roles may generate widespread shifts in welfare comparisons.

First, how about seniority–years on the job. Should this count more than it does now, count about the same as now, count less than now, or not count at all in determining a fair wage?
–Seniority–years on the job?
–Skill and ability at doing the job–should this count more or less than now?
–Education?
–How much responsibility the job entails?
–Effort made on the job?
–Importance of the job to society and the community?

Responses to these questions are shown in Table 5.1. These data demonstrate a widespread support for a continuation, if not a strengthened system, of allocating work incomes based on differences in individual productivity. Performance related standards, such as skill, ability, and effort, clearly prevailed over those not strictly performance related, such as seniority and education. Two in every three U.S. workers in 1973 favored increased reliance on performance related criteria, and just one in 20 workers felt skill, effort, or job responsibility should count less than they do now in determining a fair wage. In contrast, only two in five workers felt education and seniority should count more than they do now, and were partially offset by another one in five who said they should count less. Among all criteria, more respondents felt the current role of education and seniority in determining fair wages should be diminished. Whereas only one in 20 workers thought skills should count less, fully 20 percent felt educational attainment should count less than it does now.

Skill and effort are inputs uniquely linked to the individual, whereas education and seniority are more descriptive of differences between groups of workers. It is perhaps to be expected, then, that those criteria more descriptive of individual circumstance, and more dependent on factors within the workers' control, hold stronger appeal than general characteristics such as education and seniority. Nonetheless, this diminished role is surprising, given both the strong emphasis on education as a means for advancement and the central role seniority plays in determining wage levels. Alternatively, these data may suggest that the greater awareness in recent years of barriers to individual advancement may have resulted in workers viewing seniority and educational credentials as reflecting in part past disadvantages, and that therefore these criteria are viewed as illegitimate guidelines.

Table 5.1 also reveals that the support accorded the productivity criteria–skill, ability, and work effort–was widespread across diverse socioeconomic subgroups. The pervasiveness of this social norm was attested by the lack of divergent opinions across income, age, education, occupation, race, and sex subgroups. This similarity in normative views was especially evident in responses to the items representing individual skill, effort, and job responsibility. Agreement was somewhat less widespread on the importance of seniority, education, job

TABLE 5.1

Preferred Criteria for Judging Fairness in Pay Distribution within Major Population Subgroups, 1973
(percent of respondents who say criteria should count more, the same, or less as compared to now)

	Skill and Ability			Effort			Responsibility			Importance			Education			Seniority			
Subgroup	More	Same	Less	More	Same	Less	More	Same	Less	More	Same	Less	More	Same	Less	More	Same	Less	Cases
All respondents	79	16	5	74	21	5	66	30	4	43	45	12	38	42	20	37	45	18	811
Sex/race	78	15	7	74	21	5	65	31	4	40	47	13	37	40	23	31	46	23	428
Male/nonwhite	87	9	4	75	21	4	66	30	4	45	40	15	55	32	13	60	30	10	47
Female/white	80	17	3	74	21	5	67	28	5	44	46	10	32	49	19	38	49	13	265
Female/nonwhite	78	20	2	69	24	7	64	33	3	61	28	11	60	36	4	56	31	13	54
Occupation																			
Professional/technical	82	17	1	70	26	4	71	26	3	54	37	9	38	43	19	22	49	29	138
Managers and officials	75	18	7	72	25	3	67	31	2	35	54	11	37	42	21	23	55	22	102
Clerical and sales	83	15	2	76	19	5	68	29	3	39	49	12	33	50	17	33	49	18	165
Craftsmen and foremen	81	11	8	78	17	5	67	26	7	44	42	14	40	41	19	42	43	15	133
Operatives	75	19	6	68	24	8	57	37	6	40	45	15	42	39	19	49	38	13	134
Laborers/service	78	16	6	76	17	7	60	36	4	45	44	11	41	35	24	52	37	11	111

Income																			
Less than $5,000	81	16	3	76	19	5	66	29	5	48	41	11	40	41	19	44	43	13	234
$5,000-7,499	78	14	8	71	24	5	63	33	4	43	45	12	34	42	24	36	47	17	131
$7,500-9,999	77	17	6	75	17	8	67	27	6	45	42	13	40	35	25	39	47	14	125
$10,000-12,499	73	20	7	75	21	4	60	37	3	45	43	12	38	56	6	37	45	18	89
$12,500-14,999	77	18	5	64	33	3	62	36	2	43	39	18	39	37	24	33	44	23	61
$15,000 or more	82	15	3	71	25	4	73	25	2	31	56	13	32	47	21	16	53	31	100
Age																			
18-24	77	16	7	73	20	7	61	33	6	38	48	14	41	40	19	31	46	23	151
25-34	81	14	5	73	23	4	66	30	4	46	41	13	34	41	25	32	44	24	204
35-44	86	13	1	79	16	5	68	28	4	39	47	14	39	40	21	37	45	18	152
45-54	76	19	5	73	22	5	67	29	4	43	50	7	37	46	17	40	46	14	159
55-64	74	18	8	65	28	7	62	34	4	46	40	14	42	44	14	45	46	9	101
Education																			
9-11 grades or less	82	12	6	71	22	7	61	34	5	49	36	15	40	39	21	54	35	11	72
High school	78	16	6	75	21	4	64	32	4	39	49	12	35	47	18	38	49	13	157
Some college	77	17	6	74	20	6	70	27	3	36	56	8	39	38	23	26	51	23	132
College or advanced degree	82	17	1	72	26	2	72	27	1	55	32	13	41	40	19	15	48	37	65

Note: See Tables A1–A2 for the percentage differences required for significance.

responsibilities, and the importance of the work to the community. Support for these criteria was somewhat more contingent on individual circumstance.

Young workers were more likely to feel that seniority should count less, while those with less education wanted seniority to count more in determining wages. The older workers as well as those with little education would both benefit from a greater reliance on seniority as a criterion for income increases. In contrast, there was no systematic relationship between the respondent's own education and the emphasis placed on education as a criterion for wage differentials. Nonwhite workers were more likely to stress both education and seniority—characteristics of the person that are independent of the immediate work situation. Perhaps because of discrimination, nonwhites showed a greater predisposition toward those criteria that are less subject to bias interpretation, and more easily monitored and controlled through regulations. The importance of work to society and job responsibility were given more weight by those in professional occupations, and generally among workers with college degrees. These results plausibly reflect the impact of self-interest on the selection of criteria for judging wage equity. Overall, however, widespread and uniform support best characterizes these responses, rather than polarized views based on individual circimstance.

Referent of Comparison

More often, members of one's own occupation, and those in occupations to which people can turn if discontent, serve as referents for evaluating our current terms of trade of inputs for rewards. They shape income expectations as well as personal aspirations. Wage comparisons relate one occupation's terms of trade to another; a series of such comparisons, both in parallel and in tandem, fix our perception of relative economic position.

In this schema, people are expected to bring into consonance their internal evaluations with social reality. Yet some may choose certain outcomes of comparative evaluations in preference to others not on the basis of any distributional criteria, but simply in order to maintain a self-serving identity. With self-esteem so closely tied to the work role, especially for men, people may tend to select referents to whom they compare favorably. Such dispositions can be viewed as a characteristic of individual personality; according to dissonance theory, people tend to choose that which is most consonant with preexisting beliefs, goals, and needs.[8] Such a favorable bias is bounded, however, by a dominant preference for similar others as referents; it is this type of comparison that is most salient, regardless of its outcome.[9] Yet, the more similar the referent, the greater the consequence unfavorable comparisons have on self-esteem. As a result, we can expect people to more frequently select income referents that do not greatly threaten self-esteem through comparative disadvantage. The range of possible comparisons is thereby limited.[10]

Counteracting this favorable bias, a sense of deprivation may itself promote comparisons that justify demands for higher wages, especially unfavorable between-group comparisons. Here self-esteem is less at stake, as the focus of comparison is at the group level rather than on individual achievement. Moreover, such unfavorable comparisons are not only less denigrating, but they may even facilitate wage demands. For example, a sense of deprivation with current living standards may in turn promote unfavorable wage comparisons that are consistent with these very aspirations for higher consumption. Here relative consumption aspirations are translated into relative wage demands. Indeed, this scenario is most suggestive of the motivation behind Duesenberry's analysis.[11]

Combined, these trends suggest that selection of within-group referents may reflect a favorable bias, while choice of referent across groups may at times incorporate a bias toward unfavorable comparisons. Consistent with this interpretation is the fact that fraternalistic deprivation is reported more frequently than unfavorable evaluations stemming from within-group comparisons in each of the three surveys (see Table 4.1).

Estimates of Income Deprivation

What variables should be included as proxies for empirical estimates of differences in inputs? Based on the preceding analysis, two alternate specifications of the referent income estimation equation were contrasted (see equation 5.2 above). The first specification restricted consideration to only those income differences related to skill, experience, work time, and effort; income differentials based on characteristics or criteria other than productive efficiency were held inadmissible. Consequently, this hypothesis implies that differences in income attributable to factors such as sex, race, or geographic location directly affect people's sense of distributional equity, rather than representing adjustments in their standard of comparison. Including these characteristics would, in effect, neutralize such income differentials when making interpersonal comparisons. Furthermore, this approach holds that income evaluations are responsive to only broadly defined input classifications, not to small or marginal differences in inputs as captured by years of formal education, age, or work experience.

The alternate specification attempts to extract maximum interindividual variance stemming from market assessment and self-assessment. It adopted the hypothesis that people base their comparisons on referents that most resemble their own situation, including differences in demographic characteristics not strictly related to productivity. Thus, according to this view, people are likely to take not only abilities and experience into account, but also factors such as sex, race, geographic location, union membership, and other like characteristics. Here similarity or referent to self is viewed as crucial to the comparison process. Consequently, maximum classificatory detail on input characteristics was aimed for since it enabled greater delineation of referent (expected) incomes, and hence comparative position.

Multiple Classification Analysis (MCA), a form of a dummy variable regression, was used to estimate the additive adjustments (a_x) that represent the effect of the contribution of inputs on comparative income standards.[12] Proxies for input factors such as age/experience have demonstrated nonlinear relationships in previous research; other proxies for differences in inputs included here are categorical, having no natural scale of measurement.[13] In allowing for nonlinear relationships through multiple categorization, MCA provides an efficient analysis tool on both counts.

Table 5.2 lists the variables used as predictors in each of these equations. Since work income is the product of wage rate and time input, the inclusion of a

TABLE 5.2

Multiple Classification Analysis of Labor Income, 1973 (in dollars)

	Equation A				Equation B			
Predictor	Class Mean	Coefficient	Adjusted Mean	Cases	Class Mean	Coefficient	Adjusted Mean	Cases
Sex/race								
Male/white	11640	-1180	10892	419				
Male/nonwhite	7380	-418	8594	46				
Female/white	5568	-2803	6209	239				
Female/nonwhite	4950	-1971	7041	50				
(Beta)			(.310)					
Age/experience								
18-24	4885	-3175	5837	150	6770	-2262	6750	355
25-34	8149	-1317	7695	205				
35-44	10670	1770	10782	153	10598	1710	10722	323
45-54	10532	1860	10872	170				
55-64	14313	2622	11634	56	12764	3425	12437	72
65 and older	7344	402	9414	16				
(Beta)			(.300)				(.312)	
Education								
9-11 grades or less	7275	-1714	7298	70	6845	-2255	6757	209
High school	8551	19	9032	144	8546	-110	8902	288
Some college	9671	449	9461	124	9671	613	9630	124
College or advanced degree	13655	2750	11762	66	13655	3873	12885	66
(Beta)			(.211)				(.274)	

Average weekly work time								
30 hours or less	4131	-2192	6820	61	4131	-4183	4829	61
31-39 hours	8070	-342	8670	64	8070	-1111	7901	64
40 hours	7938	-480	8532	303	7938	-917	8095	303
41-48 hours	8325	-605	8407	124	8325	-188	8824	124
49-56 hours	12950	1985	10997	109	12950	3189	12201	109
57 hours or more	13918	2375	11387	81	13918	4048	13060	81
(Beta)			(.194)				(.330)	
Occupation								
Professional/technical	11755	1038	10050	140	11755	258	9270	140
Managers and officials	13179	1763	10775	95	] 9614	303	9315	243
Clerical and sales	7326	330	9342	148				
Craftsmen and foremen	10016	-459	8553	128	10016	1385	10397	128
Operatives	7063	-1001	8011	127	] 6330	-1308	7704	218
Laborers/service	4437	-2157	6855	91				
(Beta)			(.169)				(.137)	
Self-assessed job skill								
Low	7341	-694	8318	201				
Medium	9397	84	9096	380				
High	10294	861	9873	165				
(Beta)			(.100)					
Union membership								
Member	9868	1074	10086	180				
Nonmember	8743	-337	8675	574				
(Beta)			(.086)					
Region								
West	10606	650	9662	125				
North Central	9305	-63	8449	201				
Northeast	9581	506	9518	176				
South	7590	-626	8386	252				
(Beta)			(.073)					
Multiple RSQD (adjusted)			.436				.325	

measure of differences in average weekly work time focuses attention on wage rate comparisons. The included measure of work experience differed by sex: for men, age was used to denote years of labor force experience; female respondents were questioned as to how many years, in total, they have been employed, discounting any time during which they were not active members of the labor force. After taking account of average age at completion of schooling, these measures were combined into one scale. In addition to the level of formal education, the more detailed equation contained a measure of self-assessed job skill, and classification by sex, race, union membership, and geographic location of residence. The shorter version contained not only fewer classificatory variables, but also fewer subclasses: three rather than six age/experience categories; five instead of eight education categories, grouping together all those with less than a high school diploma, those with a diploma, and those having a diploma plus other nonacademic training but no college. The occupational classification combined managers and business officials with clerical and sales workers, semiskilled and unskilled blue-collar workers, leaving four instead of six occupation classes.

Table 5.2 displays the unadjusted class means for each variable together with the class coefficient (adjusted deviation from the grand mean) and the adjusted class mean. The grand mean ($9,012) plus the class coefficient equals the adjusted class mean. These adjusted coefficients for each predictor variable are estimates of the effect of that predictor alone, all others held constant. These coefficients are estimates of the a_x weights of equation 5.2, and thus represent the net adjustments made on overall mean income for the determination of referent or expected income. The weighted mean of the coefficients among the subclasses of each variable is zero by definition, allowing these coefficients to be interpreted with respect to the overall mean rather than deviations from an omitted subclass as is the way most dummy variable regressions are set up. The multiple correlation coefficients are adjusted for degrees of freedom and represent the percent of variance explained by the predictors aggregated, after adjustments were made for fitting the model to the particular sample being analyzed. The beta statistic is a measure of the relationship between a predictor and the dependent variable, holding constant all other predictors, and indicates the net impact of the various predictors on level of earned income. Comparisons of the magnitude of individual beta coefficients, however, must be made with caution: the rank order of betas is useful only for indicating the relative importance of the various predictors.

Each of these fitted equations accounted for a relatively large portion of observed cross-sectional variance. The more detailed equation accounted for 44 percent of the total variance, one third more than did the shorter version (33 percent). When included, the sex/race classificatory variable was rated the most important predictor by size of beta; when excluded, average weekly work time was most important. For both estimates, age/experience attained the next largest beta statistic, followed by education. The work-time variable was most affected by the inclusion of the additional variables, going from the first to the fourth-ranked predictor. Most of this swing can be associated with the presence of the sex/race variable: most males in the sample were employed at least full time; females much more often reported part-time paid employment. The inclusion of union membership may well be behind the shift in the blue-collar coefficients, making the difference between the skilled and unskilled blue-collar workers most dramatic.

From these fitted equations both measures of deprivation were calculated according to equations 5.1 and 5.3. Presented in Table 5.3 are the zero-order Pearson correlation coefficients among the deprivation measures generated from each estimate of expected income, together with their correlations with observed income itself. The two estimates of individual deprivation are correlated at r = .903, and the measures of fraternal deprivation at r = .858 (see triangle, Table 5.3). The modest correlation between GD_A and ID_B, r = .22, results from the differing estimates of expected income and represents the overlap of the relatively larger fraction of explained variance from the more detailed A estimates that is now left unexplained by the B estimates.

TABLE 5.3

Correlations among Alternate Constructed Measures of Income Deprivation (1973 data; number of cases = 811)

Measure	ID_A (1)	GD_A (2)	ID_B (3)	GD_B (4)	Y (5)
(1) $ID_A: Y - \hat{Y}_A$	1.000				
(2) $GD_A: \hat{Y}_A - \overline{Y}$	.000	1.000			
(3) $ID_B: Y - \hat{Y}_B$	.903	.220	1.000		
(4) $GD_B: \hat{Y}_B - \overline{Y}$	.000	.858	.000	1.000	
(5) $Y - \overline{Y}$	.733	.680	.812	.584	1.00

Note: Y = earned income; $\overline{Y}$ = mean sample income; $\hat{Y}_A$ = expected income based on equation A, Table 5.2; $\hat{Y}_B$ = expected income based on equation B, Table 5.2.

Differences of actual from expected income represent unexplained deviations from the mean income while the difference between expected and mean income is what is explained by the income equations. This was empirically demonstrated by their correlations with observed income itself (see rectangular boxes, Table 5.3). There we find, for the correlations involving the A estimates, that

$$(r_{1.5})^2 + (r_{2.5})^2 = 1,$$
$$(.773)^2 + (.680)^2 = 1;$$

and

$$(r_{3.5})^2 + (r_{4.5})^2 = 1,$$
$$(.812)^2 + (.584)^2 = 1,$$

derived from the B estimates. The correlation of income with individual deprivation represents the partial correspondence of income differences based on the productivity rule with whether respondents' actual income levels were above or below average. In contrast, the correspondence of estimated group deprivation with the level of observed income reflects a common criterion: for each overall mean, income serves as the comparative income standard. Their distinctiveness lies in whether transitory fluctuations in income—temporary divergences from expected income—are taken into account when making comparative income evaluations. As constructed, the measure of group deprivation discounted the impact of such temporary fluctuations.

How does one select one set of estimates over another? Two empirical tests can give guidance. First, analysis can compare the zero-order correlations of each of these estimates with the respondents' own subjective income evaluations. If the added detail included in the one set of estimates does not enhance these correlations, the less complex version would be preferred. Second, since the major difference between these estimates involves whether sex was used as a determinant of referent income, how these estimates correlate for men and women separately is of interest since systematic differences within these subgroups would help to distinguish them.*

Presented in Table 5.4 are the correlations between the various constructed measures of relative deprivation and the respondents' own reports of income evaluations previously noted. For the total sample of workers, as well as for male and female workers separately, each version obtained very similar correlation coefficients with the respondents' own self-reports. Given that no systematic differences between the two sets of estimates prevailed, Ockham's principle clearly suggests a preference for the more compact version.†

---

*This same type of analysis strategy was also employed in a multivariate context. To do this, the regression equations given in Tables 6.1–6.2 were reestimated using each version of input specifications (as well as estimates based on earnings equations using the log of annual income as the dependent variables). The results were essentially the same as those reported here.

†The standard human capital model is usually presented in terms of the relation between input variables and proportional differences in earnings, such as the log of full-time earnings. The presumption is that the earnings equation is better specified if logarithms rather than natural numbers are used for the dependent variable, since the assumptions about error distributions are more likely to be satisfied with a log dependent variable than a natural number dependent variable. However, there isn't much to be gained in this case because the MCA analysis technique allows the independent variables to be completely free

TABLE 5.4

Correlations among Subjective and Objective Measures of Income Deprivation (1973 data; cases = 811)

Measure	Income Comparisons within Occupation	Income Comparisons across Occupations	Satisfaction with Family Income	Satisfaction with Standard of Living
		All Workers (811)		
DI_A	.133	.168	.177	.141
DF_A	.037	.035	.181	.107
DI_B	.131	.173	.185	.135
DF_B	.028	.012	.176	.115
Income (Y)	.122	.147	.252	.176
		Male Workers (483)		
DI_A	.135	.154	.208	.195
DF_A	.072	– .003	.231	.150
DI_B	.143	.153	.204	.197
DF_B	.047	–.014	.219	.130
Income (Y)	.143	.118	.284	.230
		Female Workers (328)		
DI_A	.153	.243	.113	.008
DF_A	–.046	–.002	.062	.074
DI_B	.116	.219	.104	–.015
DF_B	–.021	.003	.058	.094
Income (Y)	.101	.237	.176	.086

Note: Y = earned income; $\bar{Y}$ = mean sample income; $\hat{Y}_A$ = expected income based on equation A, Table 5.2; $\hat{Y}_B$ = expected income based on equation B, Table 5.2.

---

form. Moreover, when these same equations–both form A and B (Table 5.2)–were reestimated using logs, no improvement was evidenced in the correlation of these estimates with self-reported deprivation.

Some experiments were performed to assess the relative importance of each input variable separately, but little of substance was uncovered due to problems of underidentification. More constraints on the possible range of inputs relevant for comparisons (as distinct from factors that show empirical correspondence with differences in earned income) were needed than were available. Misspecification cannot be solved empirically in situations such as this, and where questions of specification involve variables that exhibit significant intercorrelations in the collected data, practical guidance is made even more difficult.

What then can be concluded from these results? There appear to be only rather broad limits on the consensus on which inputs should count and by how much. Evaluations are not very responsive to changes in estimated referent income stemming from rather large and significant variables (sex/race), as well as from those more marginal in their effect on referent income (self-assessed job skill, geographic location, and union membership), or from less detailed input classifications (education, occupation, and age/experience). It is as if the true underlying, and observed, input dimensions on which these reports of income evaluations are based correspond about equally to each set of regression variables, not that these variables taken individually reflect substantial and unique (additive) components of an input or reward criterion.

In all multivariate analyses that follow, expected income was calculated based on the predictors age/experience, education, occupation, and work time (see equation B in Table 5.2). This same analysis was replicated for the 1974 and 1975 surveys, although not all variables included in the 1973 analysis were available in subsequent years. Similar results were drawn from each survey. Contained in Table 5.5 are the regression equations estimating expected or referent income for the 1974 and 1975 surveys.

Aspirations, Expectations, and Income Evaluations

The above empirical model of income deprivation was responsive mainly to the conditions under which wage rates are set and changed, not prices. While changes in the general price level are assumed to affect wage incomes equally, rates of inflation in excess of income change nonetheless stimulate need for income advancement and so prompt unfavorable comparisons. Moreover, as George Katona has long stressed, while inflation is widely viewed as an inequitable reduction of real personal income, subsequent (or prior) wage increases are commonly viewed as wholly earned, not partly as an inflationary adjustment. This asymmetry of response also helps promote unfavorable comparisons. And, given the high rates of inflation during the time these data were collected, its impact on these income evaluations cannot be discounted. Furthermore, these considerations suggest that income or material aspirations may affect the outcomes of comparative evaluations. Where aspirations for income advancement

TABLE 5.5

Multiple Classification Analysis of Labor Income, 1974-75
(in dollars)

	1974				1975			
Predictor	Class Mean	Coef-ficient	Adjusted Mean	Cases	Class Mean	Coef-ficient	Adjusted Mean	Cases
Age/experience								
18-34 years	7591	-2212	7490	387	9014	-2040	8796	334
35-54	11823	1875	11577	327	12969	1954	12791	276
55 and older	10703	1936	11638	123	11045	1357	12194	105
(Beta)			(.275)				(.234)	
Education								
9-11 grades or less	7215	-2966	6736	171	8966	-2176	8661	170
High school	8850	-692	9009	311	9710	-1106	9731	268
Some college	9582	480	10182	168	10513	528	11365	137
College or advanced degree	12023	2092	11793	67	16117	4465	15303	70
(Beta)			(.294)				(.282)	
Average weekly work time								
30 hours or less	4585	-4195	5507	85	5788	-4486	6351	59
31-39 hours	8183	-1696	8006	82	7869	-2787	8050	78
40 hours	9040	-408	9294	367	9192	-1201	9634	290
41-48 hours	11091	1138	10840	148	12151	801	11638	114
49-56 hours	12992	2620	12322	92	14632	3389	14226	104
57 hours or more	14795	4166	13868	61	17544	5699	16535	69
(Beta)			(.284)				(.346)	
Occupation								
Professional/technical	12349	-71	9630	132	13229	-592	10245	132
Managers/officials/clericals/ sales	10735	594	10296	322	11973	819	11655	237
Craftsmen, foremen	11524	2432	12134	113	11304	1665	12502	116
Operative, service	6524	-1703	7999	246	8312	-1282	9555	218
(Beta)			(.184)				(.140)	
Multiple RSQD (adjusted)			.286				.275	

are great, a corresponding sense of dissatisfaction with current income may be present.

Reference standards are thus dependent on personal expectations and aspirations rooted in individual circumstances, and on system expectations based on evaluations of the larger system of which the person and his group are members. Personal expectations are most related to those closest to us; they are most important for within-group comparisons. Because these expectations are central to personal identity, there is a tendency to set standards to which we compare favorably. System expectations, on the other hand, affect our broader view. Aggregate changes in prices, employment, and productivity, as well as distributional preferences, influence between-group comparisons. Here people can more easily assert comparative disadvantage in hopes of greater financial gain. Finally, intertemporal comparisons that give rise to dissatisfaction draw people's attention to the income gains of other groups; they are more receptive to seeing themselves at comparative disadvantage.

A more complete analysis of the interpersonal income comparisons would supplement the above empirical model of income differences based on input characteristics by incorporating the role of personal aspirations as well as system expectations. Their role in shaping income evaluations is not secondary; in addition to serving to ameliorate or intensify existing discrepancies, they may play an important independent role in shaping income comparisons. Consequently, analysis needs to sort out the interrelated impacts from these several sources of deprivation, including actual income differences, individual circumstance and aspirations, and expected changes in the economy as a whole. The latter sources are of special interest because the aspirations and expectations held by very many people may change in a similar direction at the same time, and thus lead to aggregate shifts in overall income evaluations. It is to this task that analysis now turns.

NOTES

1. Lee Rainwater, *What Money Buys: Inequality and the Social Meanings of Income* (New York: Basic Books, 1974).

2. See, for example, Gary S. Becker, *Human Capital* (New York: National Bureau of Economic Research, 1964); Jacob Mincer, "The Distribution of Labor Incomes: A Survey with Special References to the Human Capital Approach," *Journal of Economic Literature* 8 (March 1970): 1-27; Jacob Mincer, "Education, Experience and the Distribution of Earnings and Employment," in *Education, Income, and Human Behavior*, ed. F. Thomas Juster (New York: National Bureau of Economic Research, 1975), pp. 71-94.

3. But see Joan Robinson, "The Second Crisis of Economic Theory," in *American Economic Review* 62 (May 1972): 1-10, in which she contends that neoclassical distribution theory is bankrupt of meaningful content.

4. Milton Friedman, *A Theory of the Consumption Function* (Princeton: Princeton University Press, 1957); and Franco Modigliani and Richard Brumberg, "Utility Analysis

and the Consumption Function: An Interpretation of Cross-Section Data," in *Post-Keynesian Economics*, ed. Kenneth Kurihara (New Brunswick: Rutgers University Press, 1954), pp. 388-436.

5. James S. Duesenberry, *Income, Saving and the Theory of Consumer Behavior* (Cambridge: Harvard University Press, 1949).

6. John Thibaut and Harold Kelley, *The Social Psychology of Groups* (New York: Wiley, 1959).

7. Friedman, op. cit.

8. Leon A. Festinger, *A Theory of Cognitive Dissonance* (Stanford: Stanford University Press, 1957).

9. Herbert H. Hyman, "The Psychology of Status," *Archives of Psychology* 38 (1942): 15.

10. Thomas F. Pettigrew, "Social Evaluation Theory: Contingencies and Applications," in *Nebraska Symposium on Motivation: 1967*, ed. David Levine (Lincoln: University of Nebraska Press, 1967), pp. 245-46.

11. Duesenberry, op. cit.

12. Frank M. Andrews et al., *Multiple Classification Analysis: A Report on a Computer Program for Multiple Regression Using Categorical Predictors*, 2d ed. (Ann Arbor: Institute for Social Research, University of Michigan, 1973).

13. See, for example, Jacob Mincer, *Schooling, Experience and Earnings* (New York: National Bureau of Economic Research, 1974).

CHAPTER

6

DETERMINANTS OF INCOME EVALUATIONS

This chapter develops a multivariate model for the analysis of income evaluations. In order to more clearly isolate the separate influences of the various evaluative criteria on subjective income evaluations, responses to the two wage comparison questions were combined, as were the two satisfaction measures. In each case, the newly formed variable represented a multiplicative combination of the component questions.* This partition of income evaluations served a dual purpose. First, it separated items directly focused on interpersonal wage comparisons from those that inquired of people's general sense of satisfaction with their family income position. Second, this same grouping also represented the essential distinction between the two major normative standards of distributional equity—wage comparisons being tied more to an input-proportionality criteria, voiced income satisfaction being related more to income differences based on an egalitarian standard of distribution. As noted previously, wage comparisons were directly associated with income evaluation, and indirectly associated with satisfaction with living standards. Accordingly, the combined measure of satisfaction can be considered—in a path analytic sense—as dependent, in part, on the outcomes of the combined wage comparisons.

---

*A number of experiments using altenate methods to combine each pair of variables did not reveal any significant differences from the reported regression results. In addition to multiplicative and additive combinations, index scores were constructed that gave least weight to those who expressed relative deprivation on both of the paired items, most weight to those who rate themselves favorable on both, and intermediate scores to those who expressed mixed evaluations.

These combination variables not only make for a more simplified analytic structure, but given the high intercorrelation between the variables within each set (see Table 4.3), their pairwise combination reduces what would otherwise be moderate multicolinearity within each variable set. This enhanced the analytic goal of estimating the net influence of each of the two underlying evaluative criteria represented among these items, although these combination variables themselves still reflect the common underlying basis of the income evaluations, even apart from differences in normative standards (r = 0.4).

MULTIVARIATE MODEL

The determinants of income evaluations can be grouped into three different types or sets of factors: differences in relative income position, adjusted for potential differences in normative criteria; factors that affect the choice of income reference standards, apart from current income considerations; and factors that characterize individual circumstance and the state of the aggregate economy.

Relative Income Position

Four separate measures of relative income position have thus far been introduced: individual income deprivation—ID = $Y_i - \hat{Y}_i$; group income deprivation—GD = $\hat{Y}_i - \bar{Y}$; family welfare ratio—WR = $WR_i - \overline{WR}$; income change—$\% \Delta Y = \% \Delta Y_i - \overline{\% \Delta Y}$. The first two measures reflected a proportional rule of income distribution that related inputs to income levels; one measured discrepancies of current income from referent income, the other measured how much people's subgroup differed from the overall mean income. These first two together take account of all observed variance in earned income. In terms of the observed variance in income, the first represented deviations unexplained by the demographic predictors, the second recorded explained subgroup differences from average income. The third measure listed above was based on a more egalitarian norm of reward distribution that took account of family size and used equality of welfare shares as its standard.

The last measure focused on income change, and took an equality of percentage increment as the comparative referent. In part, evaluations of rates of wage change reflect preferences for particular patterns of and timing of adjustments to existing incomes. More may be desired, but not immediately expected or demanded. Conversely, people may be impatient, and unmet expectations themselves become the bases of feelings of relative deprivation. Although it is recognized that how people evaluate rates of income change may depend on their age and the market demand for their skills, no attempt was made to estimate such differential assessments.

Each of these measures of relative income position was available in all three surveys, except for the income change measure. For this variable, the 1973 survey measured wage change over the prior year, whereas the 1975 survey inquired about income change expected during the upcoming year. The 1974 survey did not include a measure of wage change. Reference or expected incomes were calculated based on the predictors age/experience, education, occupation, and work time (see equation B in Table 5.2, and Table 5.5).

Referent of Comparison

To these determinants of income evaluations, three variables were added to reflect the impact on reference choice stemming from individual aspirations, as well as from expected changes in consumer prices and the respondents' opinions on the effectiveness of government economic policy to combat inflation and unemployment. Because rates of inflation in excess of income change may stimulate need for income advancement and so prompt unfavorable comparisons, people who expect relatively high rates of price inflation may also more frequently judge their current income position unfavorably. In each survey, respondents were asked whether they expected consumer prices to increase, and if so by what amount.* Those who expected relatively large increases in prices more likely view their current income position as unfavorable, since both past and expected change influence evaluations.

Moreover, aggregate trends in prices and employment characterize the economic environment on which income evaluations in part depend. These contextual factors often have a dramatic influence on income evaluations, as when, for example, a majority of workers accept the necessity of moderating their wage demands even in the face of mounting inflationary pressure. In view of the central role of federal stabilization policy, the confidence people have in the ability of the federal government to combat rapid inflation and high unemployment, as were experienced during the 1973-1975 survey period, may have an important influence on income evaluations. Respondents were questioned as to whether they thought the government was doing a good job or a poor job in combating inflation and unemployment.† Those who felt government economic

---

*The question was as follows: "During the next 12 months, do you expect that prices in general will go up, or go down, or stay the same? (IF GO UP) How large a price increase do you expect?"

†The question was as follows: "As to the economic policy of the government–I mean steps taken in regard to inflation or unemployment–would you say the government is doing a good job, only fair, or a poor job?" For analysis, a one-zero variable was created contrasting those who rated government policy as poor (1), compared to those who said they were doing a fair or good job (0).

policy was being poorly conducted can be expected to be less confident that a collective solution is attainable—prompting greater need for individual action—and, because of the perceived failure of economic policy, they are more likely to expect the continuation of these economic hardships. In each case, lessened confidence in the government's stabilization policies may prompt a greater sense of current dissatisfaction.

Income satisfaction can be conceptualized as the psychological distance between the level of income aspirations and current accomplishment.[1] Consequently, the greater the margin of aspirations over current income, the greater the sense of dissatisfaction. Although aspirations for future material improvements do not necessarily diminish current satisfaction, the accomplishment of these desired economic goals does hold the promise of greater levels of satisfaction. Moreover, a high level of aspiration with its associated sense of current dissatisfaction may enable people to more easily assert comparative disadvantage. In the 1973 survey, respondents were asked how they would view income progress that would just match but not exceed increases in the cost of living.* This question attempted to single out aspirations for real income increases. In contrast to this rather general measure of income aspirations, the 1974 and 1975 surveys measured aspirations in terms of the concrete images of expanded consumption and improved living standards. These items asked respondents to rate the appeal or personal importance of upgrading consumer purchases of automobiles, home furnishings, and household durables, as well as expenditures for leisure time activities.†

Effect of Individual Characteristics

Differences in age, education, and occupation, apart from the associated income differences, may have a direct influence on income evaluations. The young are often hypothesized to be more dissatisfied with their incomes, often as a correlate of a more generalized disaffection and not simply of their relatively

---

*The question was: "If your wages or salary from your job would go up just enough to cover the rising cost of living, would this be very satisfactory, satisfactory, somewhat disappointing, or rather disturbing to you?" For analysis, respondents received scores ranging from 1 ("view no real income change as rather disturbing") through 5 ("satisfactory if no real income change").

†The question was: "Would you please look at this card and tell me the number which comes closest to how you would feel if you were able . . . A) to have a better car, B) to move to a more expensive home, C) to buy a new set of furniture, D) to have better household appliances, E) to spend more money on vacations and leisure time activities." Respondents were handed a card depicting a scale from 1 ("it would mean a great deal to me"), through 5 ("I would not want it").

lower income position. The motivations of professional workers are often found to be centered on nonfinancial rewards, leaving greater latitude for income differences.[2] Labor-market discrimination resulting in lower wages among women and minorities could be directly reflected in less favorable income evaluations. The multivariate model accordingly included the predictors age (scaled in years) and education (years), and dummy variables representing occupation (blue-collar = 1, 0 otherwise), and sex/race subgroups (with white males the omitted category).

Regression Analysis

To systematically investigate the bases of income evaluations, the two combined measures of self-reported wage comparisons and income satisfaction were regressed on the three sets of factors detailed above. For each of the three surveys, these regressions are displayed in Tables 6.1-6.2 in a stepwise fashion. The first equation in each regression set included the two estimates of individual and group income deprivation. Combined, these variables account for all of the observed variance in actual wage incomes. The second regression in each set broadened the relative income concept by the inclusion of the family welfare ratio, a more sensitive measure of deprivation when based on egalitarian standards. The third regression in each set added the influence of expected price and income change. The fourth equation added the influence of factors expected to affect the outcome of evaluations, beyond measured income differences. For the analysis of self-reported income satisfaction, a fifth equation completed the analytic model by adding the intervening impact of wage comparison on income satisfaction.

These regression equations provided the appropriate statistical evidence to evaluate both direct and indirect paths through which relative income position was translated into a sense of wage equity and more generalized economic satisfaction. All regressions were significant, although some did not account for a large proportion of observed cross-sectional variance. More importantly, however, the patterns of coefficients do lend further insight into the income-evaluation process.

An examination of the first equation in each set revealed that estimated individual income deprivation was significantly related to both types of income evaluations, while group income deprivation demonstrated a significant impact only on the more broadly based income and standard of living satisfaction. Thus, when respondents were asked to evaluate their relative wage, only divergences of actual income from expected income (based on demographic characteristics) were predictive of these evaluations. This distinction held up in each of the three surveys. For the more broadly based satisfaction measures, both individual and group deprivation mattered. Income satisfaction was thus responsive to both the

TABLE 6.1

Multivariate Regression Analysis of the Determinants of Interpersonal Wage Comparisons, among U.S. Workers, 1973-75

Independent	1973				1974				1975			
Variable	(1)	(2)	(3)	(4)	(1)	(2)	(3)	(4)	(1)	(2)	(3)	(4)
Individual income	.179	.111	.155	.166	.206	.210	.210	.216	.186	.187	.061	.067
deprivation	(5.18)	(2.78)	(3.85)	(3.88)	(6.21)	(5.21)	(5.21)	(4.74)	(5.29)	(4.16)	(1.00)	(1.05)
Group income deprivation	.035	-.024	.009	-.022	-.030	-.027	-.027	-.066	.064	.065	-.032	-.039
	(1.02)	(0.63)	(0.24)	(0.44)	(0.90)	(0.75)	(0.75)	(1.30)	(1.82)	(1.62)	(0.63)	(0.67)
Family welfare ratio		.145	.145	.113		-.007	-.006	-.033		-.002	.007	-.021
		(3.30)	(3.35)	(2.56)		(0.16)	(0.15)	(0.72)		(0.03)	(0.14)	(0.40)
Income change			.153	.132			NA*	NA			.182	.197
			(4.34)	(3.67)							(2.97)	(3.16)
Expected price change			-.111	-.089			.011	-.024			.024	.038
			(3.26)	(2.62)			(0.33)	(0.73)			(0.68)	(1.03)
Aspirations (1 = high)				-.157				-.066				-.050
				(4.51)				(1.83)				(1.32)
Economic policy (1 = poor)				.030				-.111				-.054
				(0.87)				(3.32)				(1.49)
Age (years)				.009				-.015				.013
				(0.22)				(0.34)				(0.32)
Education (years)				.010				.059				-.062
				(0.24)				(1.26)				(1.37)
Occupation (1 = blue-collar worker)				.095				-.026				-.076
				(2.31)				(0.66)				(1.76)
Sex/race												
1 = male nonwhite				.048				-.017				-.017
				(1.40)				(0.50)				(0.46)
1 = female white				.003				-.021				.017
				(0.07)				(0.49)				(0.40)
1 = female nonwhite				-.109				-.059				(0.03)
				(2.97)				(1.59)				(0.03)
Constant	6.36	5.52	4.69	4.30	5.88	5.93	5.90	5.88	6.70	6.71	5.77	7.31
SEE	3.92	3.90	3.83	3.75	3.57	3.58	3.58	3.54	3.90	3.90	3.88	3.88
RSQD (adjusted)	.031	.043	.074	.112	.041	.040	.039	.058	.036	.035	.044	.048

*An income change variable was not available in the 1974 survey.

Note: Table entries are standardized beta coefficients, with associated t-statistics in parentheses. In all cases, a positive coefficient indicates that relatively low economic status as measured by the independent variables was associated with a greater sense of income deprivation.

TABLE 6.2

Multivariate Regression Analysis of the Determinants of Reported Income Satisfaction, among U.S. Workers, 1973-75

Independent	1973					1974					1975				
Variable	(1)	(2)	(3)	(4)	(5)	(1)	(2)	(3)	(4)	(5)	(1)	(2)	(3)	(4)	(5)
Individual income	.198	.077	.104	.122	.071	.250	.121	.121	.130	.081	.269	.127	.031	.009	-.002
deprivation	(5.84)	(1.98)	(2.65)	(2.96)	(1.81)	(7.74)	(3.14)	(3.13)	(3.11)	(1.96)	(7.91)	(2.97)	(0.54)	(0.17)	(0.03)
Group income deprivation	.181	.074	.095	.080	.086	.162	.077	.077	.059	.074	.177	.080	.008	-.036	-.030
	(5.33)	(1.96)	(2.50)	(.161)	(1.84)	(5.01)	(2.21)	(2.20)	(1.28)	(1.65)	(5.21)	(2.12)	(0.16)	(0.69)	(0.57)
Family welfare ratio		.260	.260	.228	.194		.245	.245	.209	.217		.248	.250	.195	.198
		(6.13)	(6.17)	(5.34)	(4.75)		(5.93)	(5.91)	(4.96)	(5.30)		(5.35)	(5.44)	(4.23)	(4.38)
Income change			.093	.087	.047			NA*	NA	NA			.166	.199	.166
			(2.71)	(2.51)	(1.41)								(2.88)	(3.55)	(3.00)
Expected price change			-.078	-.045	-.018			-.004	.012	.006			-.102	-.088	-.094
			(2.35)	(1.38)	(.058)			(0.13)	(0.39)	(0.22)			(3.03)	(2.68)	(2.91)
Aspirations (1 = high)				-.145	-.098				-.230	-.215				-.264	-.256
				(4.34)	(3.04)				(6.95)	(6.68)				(7.76)	(7.64)
Economic policy (1 = poor)				-.047	-.038				-.153	-.128				-.072	-.063
				(1.42)	(1.20)				(5.00)	(4.27)				(2.22)	(1.98)
Age (years)				.015	.018				-.070	-.066				.019	.017
				(0.36)	(0.45)				(1.73)	(1.70)				(0.52)	(0.47)
Education (years)				-.035	-.032				-.032	-.045				.015	.025
				(0.81)	(0.77)				(0.74)	(1.09)				(0.36)	(0.62)
Occupation				-.049	-.020				-.051	-.045				.043	.056
(1 = blue collar worker)				(1.23)	(0.52)				(1.44)	(1.31)				(1.12)	(1.47)
Sex/race															
1 = male nonwhite				-.144	-.129				-.044	-.041				-.025	-.022
				(4.31)	(4.07)				(1.41)	(1.33)				(0.73)	(0.66)
1 = female white				.029	-.028				-.032	-.027				.005	.002
				(0.72)	(0.73)				(0.81)	(0.71)				(0.12)	(0.05)
1 = female nonwhite				-.107	--.074				-.035	-.022				-.090	-.091
				(3.02)	(2.18)				(1.04)	(0.66)				(2.68)	(2.73)
Wage comparisons					.303					.229					.165
					(9.35)					(7.53)					(5.19)
Constant	22.55	18.86	17.72	16.74	13.56	23.36	19.20	19.23	27.42	23.58	24.93	21.00	20.37	22.23	19.20
SEE	9.38	9.18	9.11	8.82	8.37	9.96	9.77	9.77	9.30	9.02	9.43	9.27	9.18	8.70	8.56
RSQD (adjusted)	.070	.110	.122	.178	.258	.090	.124	.123	.205	.253	.101	.132	.148	.234	.260

*An income change variable was not available in the 1974 survey.

Note: Table entries are standardized beta coefficients, with associated t-statistics in parentheses. In all cases, a positive coefficient indicates that relatively low economic status as measured by the independent variables was associated with a greater sense of income deprivation.

fairness of that income with respect to productive inputs and to how expected group income compared to the population average (see equation 1, Tables 6.1-6.2).

Given that these two constructed measures of income deprivation represent a simple additive division of the total variation from the observed mean income, these latter relationships with voiced satisfaction were also consistent with an egalitarian criterion of reward distribution. In contrast, interpersonal wage comparisons were not. Moreover, the relative sizes of the partial beta coefficients indicate that a proportional-reward criterion was not relevant to differences in these reported satisfaction levels. Unlike those for wage comparisons, the estimated beta coefficients for individual and group income deprivation did not significantly differ from one another. Hence this partition of income variation was not of consequence for these evaluations. Support is thus lent to the notion that consumption norms, as distinct from those governing renumeration, are more egalitarian. While this may seem paradoxical in that income and consumption are but two sides of the same coin, such evaluative criteria are not inconsistent as they serve different purposes and are responsive to different social forces; both advertising and the more generalized impacts of the mass media can be seen to not only provide the needed information for comparative judgments, but also to focus more attention on consumption comparisons. Moreover, these differences in evaluative criteria reflect the dual societal goal of maintaining high levels of work motivation, largely through income differentials, while at the same time providing adequate living levels for all through consumption transfers.

This view received further support from the second equation in each set of regressions, which included the family welfare ratio as a predictor, a much more sensitive measure of income position according to egalitarian standards. For the satisfaction measures, the family's welfare ratio dominated the above measures of relative income. Of the three measures of relative income position, the family's welfare ratio was the only predictor to maintain its significant direct association with reported satisfaction in each of the three surveys. In contrast, the family's welfare ratio remained an insignificant predictor of evaluative wage comparison, except in the 1973 survey.

In the 1973 survey, the amount of their last income change demonstrated its strongest impact on workers' comparative wage evaluations. Past wage change demonstrated a smaller, more indirect impact on income satisfaction. The limited and indirect impact of past income change on income satisfaction was evidenced by its insignificant direct effect, once differences in evaluative wage comparisons were controlled (compare equations 4 and 5, 1973 data, Table 6.2). A somewhat similar pattern was observed in the 1975 data. Here the larger the expected income change, the less likely that respondents voiced comparative wage deprivation or income dissatisfaction. As in the 1973 data, income change had its largest direct impact on wage comparisons, although expected wage increases also demonstrated a significant direct link to income and standard of living satisfaction.

Perhaps because expected, rather than past, income change is more closely tied with the fulfillment or nonfulfillment of aspirations, this variable demonstrated a closer and more direct impact on income satisfaction.

Aspirations played a more significant role in the determination of income satisfaction than did wage comparisons. In each of the three surveys, income and material aspirations had a significant impact on voiced satisfaction. In comparison, income aspirations showed a significant association with evaluative wage comparisons in only the 1973 survey. Perhaps this can be attributed to the differences in the measurement of aspirations in the 1973 survey. In this survey, measured aspirations directly focused on improvements in real income position, whereas in the following two surveys aspirations were measured using concrete images of material possessions. This closer conceptual relationship between wage comparisons and aspirations for real income improvement was perhaps responsible for this more substantial association in 1973; although, it can be noted, the 1974 and 1975 data did show aspirations working in the direction of prompting more unfavorable wage evaluations. Although aspirations may have some direct effect on interpersonal wage comparisons, their major direct influence was on satisfaction with income and standard of living.

An examination of the role of expected price inflation and of opinions about government economic policy revealed that these factors demonstrated no consistent and systematic impact on either wage comparisons or income satisfaction throughout the three-year survey period. These data did not demonstrate, however, that these factors did not exert any impact on income evaluations during this time period. Inflationary expectations were significantly associated with more unfavorable wage comparisons in 1973, and with reported levels of income dissatisfaction in the 1975 survey. Confidence in government economic policy demonstrated a significant direct effect on both wage comparisons and income satisfaction in the 1974 survey. Those who felt the government was doing a poor job in combating inflation and unemployment were also more likely to voice income deprivation, no matter the normative yardstick or current income position.

In interpreting these results, it should be noted that the presence or absence of significant associations was also dependent in part on ongoing economic developments. An economic environment characterized by high levels of inflation and widespread unemployment would propel some criteria to the forefront that would not hold sway during times of rapidly growing incomes and employment opportunities. Although the entire 1973-75 period was characterized by high rates of both inflation and unemployment, concern over unemployment and government economic policy was at its greatest in late 1974 when the economy was near its recessionary low point. In 1973 inflationary expectations demonstrated a significant impact on wage comparisons, while the 1975 survey showed inflationary expectations to primarily affect income satisfaction. Opinions about economic policy directly affected both wage comparisons and income satisfaction in 1974. Perhaps the significant association of inflationary expectations in 1973 and 1975, and the significant and widespread impact of opinions about government economic policy in 1974, reflected this shifting emphasis and concern from combating inflation to unemployment as the recession deepened and then receded.

The fourth equation in each regression set adds the influence of individual circumstances on people's sense of equity or income deprivation. As shown in Tables 6.1-6.2, neither age, education, nor blue-collar employment demonstrated any significant direct relationship to the outcomes of evaluative wage comparisons or income satisfaction. Recalling that these demographic variables were used to estimate expected income, these results showed that apart from this indirect effect, differences across these demographic subgroups had no direct impact on income evaluations.

The variables reflecting the race/sex subgroups (demographic characteristics not utilized for establishing referent income) indicate that white women were no less satisfied with their income or relative wages than white males. This lack of association with felt deprivation again indicates that net income differences associated with sex were not translated into a subjective sense of felt wage deprivation. In contrast, the lack of differences in income and standard of living satisfaction voiced by white men and women was in no way surprising: in each case the respondent was evaluating family income and living standards.

Nonwhite respondents were more often significantly less satisfied than white respondents with their income and standard of living, especially nonwhite females. But this greater sense of dissatisfaction among nonwhite respondents was nonsystematic and mainly limited to income and standard of living concerns. Nonwhite respondents were no more likely than white respondents to voice unfavorable interpersonal wage comparisons, except for nonwhite females in the 1973 survey. Overall, these results seem to suggest fewer differences in subjective income evaluations across these race and sex subgroups than would be indicated by the actual income differences associated with these ascriptive characteristics.

SUMMARY

What can we conclude about the bases of income evaluations? Separate measures reflecting two distinct distributional criteria were developed and contrasted. Self-reported income evaluations were found to be responsive to both a proportional and an equal share criterion. On one hand, only divergencies of current income from expected or referent income, based on broadly defined demographic and skill classifications, were predictive of wage comparisons. Income differences between these socioeconomic subgroups were discounted when making these comparisons. Alternately, for evaluations of household living levels, judgments concerned more with relative consumption than with income position, and equal share criterion outweighed labor input considerations. Here evaluations were more dependent on household incomes, adjusted for family size and needs. Aside from the indirect impact of socioeconomic characteristics in determining income-reference standards, differences in age, education, and occupation were not associated with differences in subjective income evaluations.

This difference in evaluative standards was complementary rather than inconsistent. Since evaluative wage comparisons were found to generalize and affect income satisfaction, income differences based on a proportional input criterion can then indirectly filter through to affect the more broadly based satisfaction with material living standards. In this manner, each standard of distributional equity plays an important and unique role in determining the evolving content and meaning of comparative-income evaluations. These results are highlighted in Figure 6.1. The various determinants of income evaluations tested in the multivariate model are listed on the left, with the dependent variables arranged to the right to reflect the influence of wage comparisons on the more general income satisfaction. The major paths of influence are highlighted by the dark solid lines. The double-headed arrows to the left of the independent variables indicate their interrelationships and the indirect effects, especially via reference standards. The dashed lines indicate that a significant relationship was uncovered between this pair of variables in one or another of the surveys, but this relationship was not consistent for all three. This does not indicate that these are necessarily less important paths of influence, but that the outcomes of income evaluations may in part depend on the economic environment in which they are made, and thus vary over time.

Income aspirations as well as past and expected income change demonstrated important relationships to current income evaluations. The effects of wage changes were to an important extent mediated by subjective notions of wage equity. Income and material aspirations, on the other hand, evidenced their pirmary impact on income and standard of living satisfaction, not on interpersonal wage comparisons.

Respondents who expected relatively large increases in consumer prices voiced greater wage deprivation in 1973, and greater dissatisfaction with living standards in 1975. Even when income increases more than offset rising prices, price inflation often tends to be resented as an inequitable dilution of pay hikes believed justly deserved and won. It is no wonder then that these income and price effects demonstrated substantial impact on subjective income evaluations. Moreover, respondents who thought the federal government was doing a poor job in managing the twin problems of inflation and unemployment during the 1974-75 recession were also more likely to evaluate their own situation unfavorably. Consequently, people's own sense of dissatisfaction was either eased or exacerbated by the confidence they had in the price and employment stabilization policies undertaken by the federal government.

FIGURE 6.1

Summary Display of the Determinants of Income Evaluations

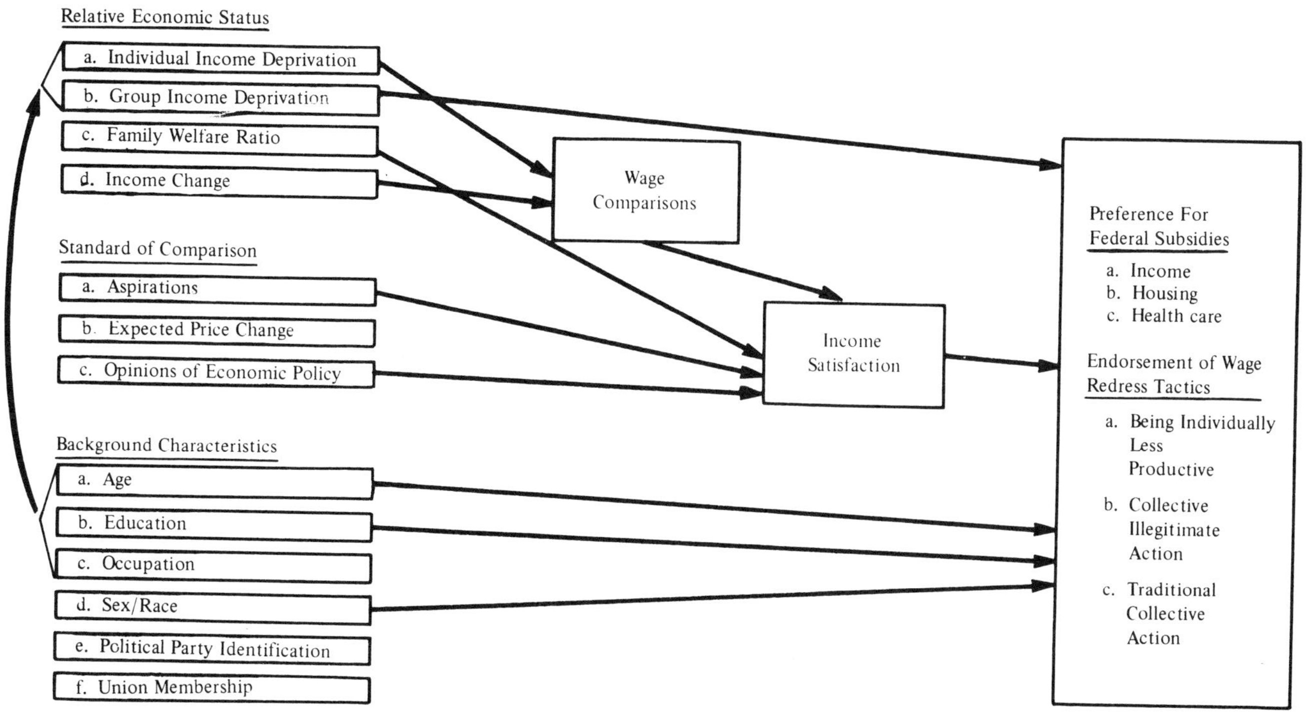

NOTES

1. Burkhard Strumpel, ed., *Economic Means for Human Needs* (Ann Arbor: Institute for Social Research, University of Michigan, 1976), chap. 1.

2. Richard Curtin, "Economic Values, Goals, and Motivations for Economic Advancement," in ibid., pp. 67-81.

CHAPTER

7

SENSE OF INTERPERSONAL DEPRIVATION: JUSTIFICATION FOR ACTION

CONSEQUENCES OF DEPRIVATION

What avenues for distributional change are open to the discontent? Foremost, they can express their demands for income redress by petition to government for a more favorable economic position established through public policy. Subsidies to individuals and groups, regulation of markets and industries, minimum wage laws, and the setting of fair conditions of employment and promotion are all intended to promote a more equitable distribution of income. Furthermore, provisions for medical care, housing, education, and other merit goods are often sought from the public sector to redress inequities because the effective distribution of economic rewards also depends on what goods and services are provided at public expense.

Atlernatively, people may choose a different route to redress inequity, which in the short run, at least, holds promise: they can bargain directly with their employer to improve their own terms of exchange of inputs for income shares. Although each group acting separately cannot for long fix the overall structure of relative wages, they can act to bolster their own wages, and thus ease their own sense of deprivation, at least for a time.

Finally, at the level of individual action, people can react to sensed deprivation with downward adjustments to their own productive inputs for their given income shares, or by demands for a greater share of income for the same level of inputs on their own part. These behaviors are least likely to effect distributional change, since the position of a particular individual in the income distribution is of more concern here than change in the size distributions of income itself, but they are nonetheless still responsive to comparative-income evaluations.

Whether the response to sensed inequity is in terms of petition to government, group action, or individual adjustment, the evolving process of distributional change is, in itself, also of crucial importance for the maintenance of social welfare. If free market mechanisms prove adequate and the government is responsive to people's claims of deprivation, whatever relative income adjustments do result will most often promote greater social welfare, if not economic efficiency. Even if extramarket mechanisms such as strikes or other forms of collective protest are utilized to gain concessions from employer or government, if these are exercised in limited and orderly fashion, social welfare is also often well served. If, however, the process is characterized by doctrinaire and unyielding demands leading to market and resource dislocation, widespread simultaneous claims for increased income shares may only lead to a situation in which there is less, in total, for all. Furthermore, demands for increased income shares, when being sought by the many, may also prompt monetary instability, especially with the inflationary push of increased wage demands. Moreover, the process and tactics used to achieve these income gains may also contribute to a lessening of the societal integration of competing economic interests. A weakened social fabric cannot but further contribute to the insistence on one's own interest over that of others. The resulting polarization can hold stability and order in economic relations in abeyance.

Here then is the core of the conflict between attainment of efficiency and equity, between market based distribution and normative judgment on distributional issues. The determination of income shares by market mechanisms leaves efficiency in resource allocation open to distortion by unmet distributional demands; conversely, if income shares are determined by normative standard, it is efficiency in resource allocation that is left vulnerable.[1] Take the energy shortage as an example. Price increases were called for, based on efficiency criteria, rationing, and price ceilings, by claims of inequity; soaring profit margins were defended as necessary to promote efficient resource development, but damned for their unjust distributional impact.

How does one choose between efficiency in resource allocation and equity in income distribution when conflicts arise, and between the need for stability and order and the need for change in an adaptive political economy? Most often, of course, it is the mix of market price mechanisms, regulation of relative market power, and government subsidies that are in question, as the attainment of each goal is sought. At times, however, one goal may be pursued to the clear detriment of another, as when strikes in basic industries cripple the productive capacity of whole economies, or when public demonstrations against established economic interests force abrupt and drastic distributional change. This choice in setting priorities is exercised in response to public demand, and increasingly norms of equity are being favored over unregulated market mechanisms. Even measures taken to counteract cyclical development in income and employment are now more often chosen on grounds of equity.

Since social welfare is not only affected by distribution itself, but also by the process of change, two facets of distributional norms are of interest for this study. First, what actions are seen as legitimate or acceptable in the pursuit of wage equity? These rules of social behavior delineate what tactics are permissible to exact distributional change. In doing so, these same social norms also limit the consequences of such actions on societal integration and economic stability.

Second, what prompts individual behavior directed toward distributional change? The determinants of income comparison suggest several factors that may stimulate change on the individual level. The following chapter investigates this link between people's sense of interpersonal equity and behavioral predisposition aimed at distributional change. There the motivational content of people's sense of equity is at issue. The present chapter gives a descriptive analysis of the norms governing the process of distributional change. Because claims of wage inequity are based on outcomes of so-called legitimate processes and institutions, the range of behaviors studied must include what, from another viewpoint, are considered illegitimate tactics to gain income concessions. Such illegitimate actions, however, are of double interest for this study because, if they are undertaken, they are also likely to have repercussions on societal integration and economic stability. Do people have the right to strike, regardless of circumstance? Are they justified in disrupting production of goods and services by work slowdowns, wildcat strikes, being less productive, or doing work poorly or incorrectly on purpose? Should protest that disrupts public order be tolerated? Respondents were directly questioned as to the appropriateness of several such reactions to wage inequity in order to investigate the normative parameters governing individual and group labor market behavior.

In addition to predispositions toward wage change, equity notions can also be expected to affect preferences for government programs that alter the distribution of income. Should the federal government directly intervene and establish a system of job and standard-of-living guarantees for all, or should each individual compete on his own, trading his own inputs for what rewards they can command in the marketplace? Should medical care and housing be provided to all at public expense? Since the egalitarian standard of distributional equity requires nonmarket distributional methods, the answers respondents gave when questioned concerning their views on what role the federal government ought to play in the provision of economic welfare are of central interest.

Accordingly, the first part of this chapter investigates people's attitudes toward various methods to redress wage inequity. Following this, analysis turns to an examination of the desired role of the federal government in the income allocation process, focusing on proposed public policies that would subsidize individual incomes and living standards. Throughout, analysis is primarily descriptive of the content and dispersion of these views across socioeconomic subgroups. This analysis is of special interest because these normative criteria not only serve as guidelines for individual behavior, but can also serve as guidelines for public policy. Consequently, whether agreement on normative criteria was widespread and uniform across diverse population subgroups, or whether there existed sharp differences and polarization was of crucial importance. The following chapter then completes the investigation of how current income evaluations, and the underlying determinants of comparisons, each act to shape these predispositions and thus motivate income redress.

PREFERRED TACTICS FOR REDRESSING WAGE INEQUITY

The most widely preferred method of redressing inequitably low wages is to seek an income increase (although, at times, proposed wage increases are viewed with public alarm, and have prompted effective restraint on what were thought to be inequitably high wage demands). Rarely are reductions in another's income advocated to bring relative wages in balance. If wages are inflexible or otherwise unresponsive to claims of inequity, the other alternative is to reduce inputs (either in quantity or quality) while maintaining the same absolute income level, relative terms of exchange being thereby enhanced.* Either strategy can be undertaken by individuals acting alone, or by groups of people seeking to defend their common interest. And either strategy could incorporate methods of change or actions that may not be widely regarded as legitimate.

What actions will people condone in order to redress wage inequities? In the 1973 and 1974 surveys, respondents were asked to rate the following actions on a five-point scale ranging from "always right" (1) to "never right" (5):

> Some people think they get *less* pay from their job than they feel they justly deserve. What would be right for them to do in this situation?
> –How about participating in union-approved strikes?
> –Not working as hard on the job?
> –Participating with co-workers in a work slow-down?
> –Asking for a pay increase?
> –Doing work poorly or incorrectly on purpose?
> –Taking longer lunch and rest breaks?
> –Quitting the job?
> –Not coming to work regularly?

*Yet another is to increase demands for nonmonetary rewards, such as job enrichment or social recognition, while maintaining otherwise constant levels of work inputs and outputs.

–Non-violent protesting like picketing?
–Participation in strikes not approved by the union?
–Protesting in public places even if it disrupts order?

Presented in Table 7.1 are the breakdowns of responses among all working respondents in the 1973 and 1974 survey. The actions are listed in order of their acceptance, as based on average scale means. The actions that conform closely to traditional market behavior, both individual ("asking for a pay increase", "quitting the job") and collective ("union approved strikes," "picketing") were more often judged as right by respondents. But note that the action "ask for a pay increase" was judged as "always right" by just over half of all respondents in each of the surveys, and for no other action do more than one third of all respondents give such unqualified support. On the other hand, approximately one in three respondents in each survey said "quitting the job" was never right. As shown later, these responses are partly explained by the social protest aspect of such action in the context of wage disputes.

Collective actions such as nonunion strikes and disruptive protests in public places found much less acceptance as these actions were more widely considered illegitimate. Less than one in 20 respondents found such actions "always right" in response to wage inequity. And the least defensible actions, according to these data, were those that involved doing work poorly or incorrectly on purpose, or irregular work attendance, all of which may be termed illegitimate individual actions. In both the 1973 and 1974 surveys, U.S. workers were nearly unanimous in the view that not coming to work regularly, or doing work poorly or incorrectly on purpose were never the right response to inequitably low wages.

Behavioral Dimensions Underlying Reactions to Inequity

Justifications for actions to remedy inequity tend to cluster, where respondents associate the methods of action, and where the actions are directed toward common ends. Table 7.2 presents the pattern coefficients from a factor analysis.[2] The factor analytic technique partitions total observed variance into that which is influenced by shared determinants, called common, and that part which is influenced by unique determinants. Variations in responses that stem from determinants unique to each particular survey item (and its associated error variance) were excluded from analysis; attention was directed to common determinants, and hence to the underlying orientations toward these labor market actions.

Separate factor analyses of the 1973 and 1974 data revealed a nearly identical dimensional structure. This similarity is highlighted in Table 7.2, which presents the parallel results for each factor analysis. This similarity across two

TABLE 7.1

How Workers Rate Various Actions Used to Redress Inequitable Pay (percentages)

Action	1973 (cases = 811)				1974 (cases = 872)			
	Always Right	Sometimes Right	Never Right	Total	Always Right	Sometimes Right	Never Right	Total
Ask for pay increase	58	37	5	100	63	33	4	100
Union strike	15	57	28	100	29	47	24	100
Picketing	16	42	42	100	20	42	38	100
Quit job	20	44	36	100	13	50	37	100
Work slowdown	7	24	69	100	5	16	79	100
Nonunion strike	3	19	78	100	4	23	73	100
Not work hard*	5	21	74	100	3	10	87	100
Take longer breaks*	2	12	86	100				
Disruptive protest	3	9	88	100	3	11	86	100
Not work regularly	2	6	92	100	1	2	97	100
Do work poorly	2	2	96	100	0	1	99	100

*These two items were merged in the 1974 survey.

TABLE 7.2

Factor Analyses of Actions Justified in the Event of Inequitable Pay

	Primary Factor Pattern					
	Actions Aimed at Being Individually less productive		Illegitimate Collective Action		Traditional Collective Action	
Variable	1973	1974	1973	1974	1973	1974
Do work poorly	.641	.750	.154	-.065	-.044	.183
Not work regular	.597	.734	.169	.111	.014	.041
Take long breaks*	.512	.294	.038	.029	.241	.604
Not work hard*	.483		-.256		.456	
Nonunion strike	.300	.117	.545	.384	.120	.288
Picketing	-.066	.011	.526	.803	.336	-.014
Disruptive protest	.222	.125	.484	.520	.137	.164
Quit job	.021	.003	.353	.248	-.090	-.105
Ask pay increase	-.262	-.074	.226	.147	.096	.073
Work slowdown	.182	.172	-.099	.103	.627	.683
Union strike	-.128	.048	.208	.494	.486	.178
Factor	Correlations Among Primary Factors					
Individual action	1.000	1.000				
Illegitimate action	0.009	0.115	1.000	1.000		
Traditional action	0.344	0.249	0.381	0.295	1.000	1.000

*These two items were merged in the 1974 survey.

independent random cross-sectional samples attests the stability of the underlying attitudinal dimensions, as represented among these items. Since the normative beliefs that underpin these views change but slowly, this measurement stability was expected, and is reassuring on methodological grounds.

The factor patterns delineate the grouping or clustering of variables. The pattern coefficients represent the direct relationship of each item to the factor representing that melange of responses. Each solution was three-dimensional, meaning that there were three common underlying sets of associations made by respondents in each survey. The correlations among the factors indicate that the first dimension (factor) obtained in each survey was distinct from the second, but less so from the third; the second and third showed moderate positive intercorrelation (see Table 7.2).

These dimensions can be interpreted by examining the pattern of factor loadings within each survey analysis (see Table 7.2). The first factor in each survey was associated most with the items that portrayed poor workmanship, irregular attendance, taking long breaks, and not working hard as responses to wage inequity. All of these actions involve adjustments at the individual level, not among workers acting in concert. And all aim to lower individual productivity rather than to increase income. Since this dimension focuses on reactions that involve being individually less productive, this first factor was so labeled.

Actions such as nonunion strikes, picketing, and disruptive protest in public places dominated the second factor. This behavioral dimension focused more on collective responses to wage inequity, incorporating what are often considered illegitimate means. That this dimension was more concerned with raising income levels, whereas the first was directed more toward lowering inputs, was attested by the loadings on the item "ask for pay increase." In the 1973 survey, voicing pay demands related negatively to justifications for becoming individually less productive, but demonstrated a positive relationship with the collective efforts to raise wages, as represented by the second dimension.

Note also that "quitting the job" was associated most with collective illegitimate actions in both surveys, indicating that in some contexts quitting can be interpreted as a protest action of questionable legitimacy. Interestingly, the variance in responses to this item and to the item "ask for pay increase" contributed least to the total common variance among the set of variables. This indicates that a greater proportion of variation in responses to these items reflected not the common concerns of collective or individual protest actions, but much more commonly accepted methods of countering individual dissatisfaction.

The third factor had its highest loadings on collective work slowdowns, union strikes, not working hard, and nonviolent picketing. Since the actions represented among these items are now widely practiced, this last orientation was accordingly labeled traditional collective action.

The positive correlation between the second and third dimension reflects their common focus on collective actions, with picketing and strike activities providing the strongest connecting links between the more traditional and those seen as less legitimate. But, the first and second dimensions, each of which represents reactions widely considered illegitimate, are uncorrelated, indicating no generalization of views across these two types of illegitimate responses. Instead, their independence indicates the juxtaposition of whether input reduction or income increases were sought to redress wage inequity. Orientations toward traditional collective actions and individual input reductions showed moderate association. Both were influenced by actions that affect level of work activity, but in one context these actions were related to the individual situation, and in the other to collective actions.

Differing Views on Wage Redress Tactics

In addition to identifying the basic behavioral dimensions underlying reactions to wage inequity, analysis needs to determine whether individual workers differ in their viewpoints. Significant differences and subgroup polarization may not only directly contribute to a sense of deprivation, but may also weaken chances for resolution without incurring excessive social and economic penalties. On the other hand, widespread agreement on acceptable tactics for redress contributes to the establishment and maintenance of a cooperative and responsive atmosphere. This helps to facilitate difficult adjustments to relative wages when circumstance warrants. It was therefore important to assess the uniformity with which these beliefs were held across social and political dimensions—as represented by political party identification, education, and age—and across lines of economic interest—as represented by income, occupation, and union membership.

To investigate individual differences, respondents were scored according to the extent of their approval of each type of reaction to inequity. A description of the three factor dimensions in terms of the measured survey items is a relatively straightforward procedure, using conventional multiple regression methods to obtain estimates of each respondent's score.* To highlight differences across socioeconomic subgroups, scale scores were rank ordered on each dimension, and partitioned into three equal subgroups. In part these tercile scores represent the range of relative support underlying most social norms. However, this measure is also sensitive to any differences in the concentration of support among particular socioeconomic subgroups, and thus can indicate the extent of polarization or uniformity of belief. Tables 7.3-7.5 report these demographic profiles for each of the three reaction dimensions, respectively. Each table documents the extent of relative approval or disapproval among subgroups for the 1973 and 1974 surveys.

Of all classifications, age and education yield the clearest distinctions. The young were more likely to endorse remedial action of all types, especially those under age 25. For each wage redress tactic, and in each survey, approval declined systematically with age.

---

*The estimates of factor scores for each respondent can be expressed as follows:

$$F = S' R^{-1} Z,$$

using the same notation as previously defined. A measure of the accuracy of estimating a factor by means of the above equation is given by its coefficient of multiple correlation. Each of the three estimated factors achieved a value of between .80 and .90 for this coefficient.

TABLE 7.3

Approval of Being Individually Less Productive to Redress Wage Inequity, among Major Population Subgroups, 1973-74 (percentages)

	1973				1974			
Subgroup	Approve	Pro-Con	Dis-approve	Cases	Approve	Pro-Con	Dis-approve	Cases
All respondents	33	34	33	811	33	34	33	872
Sex/race								
Male/white	37	30	33	435	32	36	32	440
Male/nonwhite	48	25	27	48	48	21	31	63
Female/white	25	36	39	271	29	36	35	297
Female/nonwhite	37	49	14	57	42	21	37	72
Occupation								
Professional/technical	33	34	33	143	30	34	36	135
Managers and officials	25	30	45	103	22	40	38	148
Clerical and sales	26	36	38	167	30	33	37	188
Craftsmen and foremen	38	25	37	133	32	33	35	120
Operatives	40	37	23	137	48	28	24	123
Laborers/service	40	32	28	115	38	34	28	131
Income								
Less than $5,000	35	34	31	241	38	33	29	247
$5,000-7,499	36	34	30	132	29	30	41	118
$7,500-9,999	37	36	27	128	39	35	26	124
$10,000-12,499	33	28	39	90	36	35	29	119
$12,500-14,999	30	29	41	63	21	40	39	80
$15,000 or more	23	34	43	100	25	34	41	145
Age								
18-24	45	32	23	152	44	33	23	145
25-34	33	35	32	208	36	35	29	252
35-44	29	29	42	156	26	33	41	170
45-54	30	37	33	161	29	33	38	173
55-64	32	28	40	104	25	34	41	114
Education								
9-11 grades or less	37	33	30	222	36	32	32	181
High school	34	31	35	318	29	37	34	316
Some college	28	34	38	133	33	37	30	179
College or advanced degree	33	36	31	135	36	31	33	139
Union								
Union member	38	31	31	186	38	29	33	207
Not union member	32	34	34	614	31	35	34	656
Political-party preference								
Democrat	36	32	32	430	36	32	32	473
Independent	40	27	33	146	29	38	33	176
Republican	33	34	33	221	26	36	38	213

TABLE 7.4

Approval of Illegitimate Collective Actions to Redress Wage Inequity, among Major Population Subgroups, 1973–74 (percentages)

	1973				1974			
Subgroup	Approve	Pro-Con	Disapprove	Cases	Approve	Pro-Con	Disapprove	Cases
All respondents	33	34	33	811	33	34	33	872
Sex/race								
Male/white	38	32	30	435	29	34	37	440
Male/nonwhite	42	33	25	48	48	40	12	63
Female/white	24	36	40	271	34	30	36	297
Female/nonwhite	39	30	31	57	43	37	20	72
Occupation								
Professional/technical	47	33	20	143	28	37	35	135
Managers and officials	25	35	40	103	20	32	48	148
Clerical and sales	30	35	35	167	32	30	38	188
Craftsmen and foremen	35	33	32	133	30	34	36	120
Operatives	32	29	39	137	50	31	19	123
Laborers/service	26	36	38	115	40	36	24	131
Income								
Less than $5,000	32	30	38	241	40	34	26	247
$5,000-7,499	30	36	34	132	41	28	31	118
$7,500-9,999	34	30	36	128	39	34	27	124
$10,000-12,499	37	35	28	90	37	29	34	119
$12,500-14,999	40	33	27	63	26	30	44	80
$15,000 or more	40	38	22	100	16	40	44	145
Age								
18-24	43	30	27	152	52	28	20	145
25-34	39	32	29	208	42	29	29	252
35-44	30	38	32	156	22	37	41	170
45-54	28	32	40	161	25	38	37	173
55-64	22	34	44	104	19	34	47	114
Education								
9-11 grades or less	30	30	40	222	29	38	33	181
High school	28	35	37	165	33	30	37	316
Some college	35	37	28	286	39	29	32	179
College or advanced degree	55	29	16	135	34	37	29	139
Union								
Union member	38	33	29	186	43	32	25	207
Not union member	32	33	35	614	30	33	37	656
Political-party preference								
Democrat	36	33	31	430	41	32	27	473
Independent	38	26	36	146	29	37	34	176
Republican	26	42	32	301	24	29	47	311

TABLE 7.5

Approval of Traditional Collective Actions to Redress Wage Inequity, among Major Population Subgroups, 1973-74 (percentages)

	1973				1974			
Subgroup	Approve	Pro-Con	Dis-approve	Cases	Approve	Pro-Con	Dis-approve	Cases
All respondents	33	34	33	811	33	33	34	872
Sex/race								
Male/white	37	32	31	435	32	36	32	440
Male/nonwhite	42	37	21	48	48	21	31	63
Female/white	24	33	43	271	29	36	35	297
Female/nonwhite	44	37	19	57	42	21	37	72
Occupation								
Professional/technical	36	38	26	143	38	34	28	135
Managers and officials	21	27	52	103	24	34	42	148
Clerical and sales	27	36	37	167	34	31	35	188
Craftsmen and foremen	41	32	27	133	40	32	28	120
Operatives	42	31	27	137	32	37	31	123
Laborers/service	32	31	37	115	30	30	40	131
Income								
Less than $5,000	37	29	34	241	30	33	37	247
$5,000-7,499	36	33	31	132	31	26	43	118
$7,500-9,999	35	35	30	128	35	37	28	124
$10,000-12,499	33	32	35	90	37	37	26	119
$12,500-14,999	36	29	35	63	41	33	26	80
$15,000 or more	23	38	39	100	38	28	34	145
Age								
18-24	46	32	22	152	41	36	23	145
25-34	38	32	30	208	44	32	24	252
35-44	30	36	34	156	24	34	42	170
45-54	27	34	39	161	26	33	41	173
55-64	20	31	49	104	27	29	44	114
Education								
9-11 grades or less	36	34	30	222	24	31	45	181
High school	32	33	35	318	30	36	34	316
Some college	29	32	39	133	37	31	32	179
College or advanced degree	39	34	27	135	43	33	24	139
Union								
Union member	50	27	23	186	48	28	24	207
Not union member	28	35	37	614	29	34	37	656
Political-party preference								
Democrat	39	32	29	430	40	32	28	473
Independent	32	37	31	146	34	28	38	176
Republican	23	31	46	221	20	39	41	213

Differences across educational and occupational subgroups indicate that college degree holders more often approved of the use of collective actions to redress inequitable wages. Among those with the least marketable job skills, especially operatives and service workers, reduction in individual effort to counteract wage inequity more often found acceptance. These differences may plausibly reflect economic circumstance: the unskilled have the least chance of upgrading thier pay, aside from general economywide increases, while for workers with a college degree, a nontraditional collective approach may prove more effective in winning wage increases.

Although income, occupation, and education are often used in conjunction (and often interchangeably) as indicators of socioeconomic position, differences in approval of these various means for wage redress across income subgroups were less systematic. Indeed, the 1973 data showed that higher income groups voiced greater approval for illegitimate collective responses, while the 1974 data indicated the opposite. Subsequent multivariate analysis demonstrated that this reversal in the income relationship cannot be accounted for by other correlated socioeconomic factors. The lack of a systematic relationship with income position—the most central indicator of economic position—and the strong relationship with age, and to a lesser extent education and occupation, suggest that these differences in approval across population subgroups have more to do with social than economic position.

The role of group identification, as based on shared social beliefs and daily experience, in shaping these views was also indicated. Union members were much more likely to endorse traditional collective actions in each survey, and voiced somewhat greater approval for the other tactics as well. The importance of political ideology was indicated by the association of party identification with differences in the approval of wage redress tactics. The 1973 data indicated that self-identified Republicans showed the greatest divergence in opinion from Democrats and Independents. In that year Republicans voiced relatively less approval of each type of reaction to wage inequity, while the Democrats and Independents were more similar in the extent of their endorsement. In contrast, in the 1974 survey self-identified Democrats were most distinctive in the extent of their approval, with the Independents joining the Republicans in voicing relatively less approval of each type of action. These results perhaps reflect the impact of shifting contextual factors in the political arena, although in each survey traditional collective actions found greatest support among Democrats and least among Republicans, with Independents taking a middle position. It is also of some interest to note that white females were much less likely to endorse each of the tactics for redress in 1973, but showed only small differences from white males in 1974. In both years, nonwhite respondents voiced greater approval of each type of response to wage inequity.

Many seemingly significant differences in reported proportions among particular population subgroups in the 1973 survey failed to be replicated a year later.

And some large differences in the 1974 survey were not present one year earlier. This reflects in part true underlying change, and in part survey and measurement error. Although sorting out these potential sources of change was not possible using these data alone, the data do indicate the absence of enduring and sharply polarized views. These beliefs were widely shared among diverse economic subgroups. Rather than differences and opinions being drawn along lines of economic interest, the clearest distinctions were associated with the age and education of the respondent. Although two cross-sectional measurements are not adequate to address questions of change over time, age and education are often used as indicators of potential trends in social change. However, since differences in age, education, and current income position are all interrelated, an assessment of these potential sources must await the multivariate analysis contained in the next chapter.

FEDERAL INCOME SUBSIDY PROGRAMS

In addition to predispositions toward wage change, preferences for public policies that affect the distribution of income can also be expected to reflect equity considerations. Since the egalitarian standard of distribution requires nonmarket distributional methods, preferences for federal subsidy programs depend, in part, on underlying distributional preferences, and can thus serve as guidelines for public policy. In the 1974 survey, respondents were handed a showcard detailing a five-point scale of responses ranging from placing complete responsibility on the individual for providing for family income and living standard, to holding the federal government primarily responsible for providing income security for each citizen. Respondents were then asked the following questions:

> Some people feel that the federal government should see to it that every person has a job and a good standard of living. Others think the government should let each person get ahead on his own. And, of course, other people have opinions somewhere in between. Which number comes closest to how you feel?
>
> How about medical and family health care: should the federal government see to it that every person receives adequate medical care, or should everyone be responsible for his own medical care?
>
> Some people feel the federal government should see to it that all people have adequate housing, while others feel each person should provide for his own housing. Which number comes closest to how you feel about this?

The question concerning government job and standard-of-living guarantees was asked in both the 1973 and 1974 survey.*

*While the wording of the question in the 1973 survey was nearly identical to the above quoted 1974 item, in the 1973 survey respondents were asked to use a seven-point rating scale instead of the five-point scale used in 1974.

In response, almost half of all working respondents in each survey (45 percent) said they preferred having each individual "get ahead on his own" to having the federal government "see to it that every person has a job and good standard of living" (see Table 7.6). Approximately one respondent in four preferred government intervention to individual efforts.

TABLE 7.6

Preferences for Federal Subsidy Programs (percentages)

Program	Government Responsibility		Shared Responsibility	Individual Responsibility
	1973	1974	(1974)	(1974)
Job and standard of living	29	22	28	51
Housing	24	36	32	31
Health care	47	42	40	18
Total	100	100	100	100
Cases	811	872	872	872

The remaining one in four respondents stated that they were equally drawn to each view. Interestingly, these preferences for general income guarantees did not significantly differ from year to year, although aggregate economic conditions were much worse in 1974.

Preferences for federal housing programs were quite similar to those concerning jobs and living standards. The view that individuals should provide for their own housing was held by four in ten respondents; another three in ten respondents were of the opinion that the federal government should be primarily responsible for providing adequate housing, with the remaining one in three indicating that housing responsibility should be shared. In contrast, more widespread support for government intervention in the provision of medical care was evidenced by these data. A clear majority (51 percent) felt that "the federal government should see to it that every person receives adequate medical care." Only two in ten respondents placed primary responsibility on the individual for providing medical care.

Whether these preferences as measured represent an affirmation or departure from existing federal subsidy programs cannot be ascertained. These data do indicate, however, greater public support for federal health care programs than for general income guarantees or housing subsidies. This difference in preferences reflects in part the long-standing tradition in public finance of regarding expenditures for medical care both as a social good—by virtue of the externalities involved—and as a merit good—by virtue of the special needs of the particular individuals involved.[3]

Subgroup Differences in Subsidy Preferences

How these opinions vary across age and income subgroups was of particular concern. Income is important because it represents both variations in potential individual benefits as well as in cost through individual taxation. Age reflects important differences in individual circumstance, and the horizon of expected lifetime benefits and costs of federal programs. Generally, differences in these preferences among socioeconomic subgroups will indicate whether the support for expanded income subsidies was widespread and uniformly held, or whether there existed sharp differences in the view of the proper role of the federal government. Table 7.7 reports the distribution of preferences for job and income subsidies within major demographic subgroups; Table 7.8 reports similar data on housing and health care preferences.

As shown in Table 7.7, the higher the respondent's family income, the more frequently support was voiced for individual responsibility rather than government subsidy. A majority of those with family incomes above $15,000 in each survey preferred individual to government responsibility for providing adequate jobs and housing, whereas just one in three families with incomes of $5,000 or less voiced the same opinion. In a similar fashion, low-income respondents showed a greater preference for federal housing subsidies. In contrast, smaller and less systematic differences in support of health care subsidies were evidenced across income groups by these data (Table 7.8). This lack of correspondence, as captured by the income variable, between individual costs of and benefits from a federal health care program perhaps indicates the distinctive social welfare character of this particular program.

It is interesting to note that, as might be expected, based on the above income relationships, those with unskilled occupations and little formal education would also more frequently prefer government job and income guarantees. And consistent with the previous discussion on the relatively greater importance of interpersonal wage comparisons for managerial workers, a majority of these workers in each survey also thought each individual should be primarily responsible for their own economic advancement.

The elderly, those 65 years or older, as well as the youngest respondents, under age 35, reported relatively greater support for government housing and health care subsidies. Although those over 65 were by far the most supportive of government subsidies for housing and health care, the young were more supportive of government job and standard of living guarantees. In contrast, in each survey respondents aged 35-54 were more drawn to individual responsibility

TABLE 7.7

Preferences for Federal Job and Standard of Living Subsidy Programs, among Major Population Subgroups, 1973-74
(percent of respondents who favor government or individual responsibility for adequate job and standard of living)

	1973				1974			
Subgroup	Government	Shared	Individual	Cases	Government	Shared	Individual	Cases
All respondents	29	24	47	702	22	36	42	861
Sex/race								
Male/white	21	24	55	385	16	33	51	437
Male/nonwhite	64	10	26	42	47	29	24	62
Female/white	27	29	44	222	19	42	39	295
Female/nonwhite	62	17	21	53	45	31	24	67
Occupation								
Professional/technical	29	27	44	137	21	35	44	134
Managers and officials	21	22	57	93	15	29	56	148
Clerical and sales	23	27	50	144	15	46	39	185
Craftsmen and foremen	21	25	54	112	16	35	49	118
Operatives	34	23	43	108	34	37	29	121
Laborers/service	44	18	38	97	28	31	41	128
Income								
Less than $5,000	38	27	35	202	30	38	32	243
$5,000-7,499	30	22	48	115	25	37	38	117
$7,500-9,999	28	22	50	112	20	34	46	124
$10,000-12,499	23	25	52	79	21	37	42	118
$12,500-14,999	17	29	54	57	11	43	46	80
$15,000 or more	14	19	67	93	12	30	58	145
Age								
18-24	40	22	38	127	28	40	32	145
25-34	26	27	47	187	22	37	41	248
35-44	23	25	52	137	16	33	51	170
45-54	23	24	53	139	21	29	50	170
55-64	26	22	52	87	21	41	38	111
Education								
9-11 grades or less	38	22	40	173	32	30	38	176
High school	24	28	48	271	15	40	45	313
Some college	20	22	58	122	20	32	48	179
College or advanced degree	32	22	46	133	19	44	37	138
Union								
Union member	40	22	38	156	26	36	38	205
Not union member	22	22	44	614	20	36	44	647
Political-party preference								
Democrat	39	21	40	197	27	37	36	185
Independent	26	25	49	165	20	38	42	307
Republican	12	26	62	329	11	31	58	363

TABLE 7.8

Preferences for Federal Housing and Health Care Subsidy Programs, among Major Population Subgroups, 1974 (percent of respondents favoring)

	Responsibility for Health Care				Responsibility for Housing			
Subgroup	Government	Shared	Individual	Cases	Government	Shared	Individual	Cases
All respondents	50	32	18	856	28	32	40	861
Sex/race								
Male/white	47	31	22	431	20	31	49	436
Male/nonwhite	77	13	10	61	56	25	19	61
Female/white	46	38	16	295	25	35	40	296
Female/nonwhite	67	26	7	69	59	34	7	68
Occupation								
Professional/technical	56	25	19	134	22	33	45	134
Managers and officials	44	37	19	146	21	28	51	148
Clerical and sales	46	35	19	185	28	32	40	187
Craftsmen and foremen	48	31	21	117	23	37	40	117
Operatives	59	27	14	118	34	32	34	119
Laborers/service	50	36	14	129	34	34	32	129
Income								
Less than $5,000	52	34	14	245	35	33	32	245
$5,000-7,499	48	37	15	115	27	38	35	118
$7,500-9,999	54	31	15	123	26	39	35	123
$10,000-12,499	53	26	21	118	30	25	45	117
$12,500-14,999	48	35	17	77	20	27	53	80
$15,000 or more	45	26	29	143	17	28	55	144
Age								
18-24	59	29	12	145	37	34	29	145
25-34	57	27	16	250	33	35	32	251
35-44	43	32	25	166	23	28	49	167
45-54	42	38	20	169	21	28	51	169
55-64	47	38	15	110	17	36	47	112
Education								
9-11 grades or less	52	37	11	175	34	29	37	176
High school	47	33	20	312	25	32	43	314
Some college	48	34	18	176	25	35	40	178
College or advanced degree	59	19	22	138	27	30	43	138
Union								
Union member	57	26	17	202	33	27	40	202
Not union member	49	33	18	646	26	34	40	651
Political-party preference								
Democrat	57	30	13	431	32	33	35	236
Independent	54	29	17	266	28	35	37	273
Republican	38	34	28	153	18	27	55	346

rather than to government intervention. Female respondents were similar to males in their preferences for government health care subsidies, but less willing to rely solely on individual responsibility for providing adequate housing and material living standards. Nonwhite respondents, of both sexes, voiced significantly greater support for health care, housing, and job and income subsidies. These differences plausibly mirror individual circumstances and life-cycle changes in family needs and income.

Preferences for federal subsidy programs represent more than just socioeconomic position and comparisons of costs to benefits; they also reflect differences in normative views apart from self-interest. Respondents who identified themselves as Republicans were much more likely to endorse individual responsibility. Self-identified Democrats were more drawn toward the view that the federal government is responsible for providing adequate health and material living standards. But these differences in ideological views were not extreme. Except for health care subsidies, a majority of Republicans voiced a preference for individual responsibility; in contrast, only for the health care program did a majority of Democrats favor government subsidies. And, although the sharpest differences were noted in job and income subsidy preferences, more than one in three Democrats nonetheless favored individual over government responsibility.

SUMMARY

This chapter explored two avenues through which individuals can seek income redress. The first involves individual and collective labor market tactics, the second concerns the role of federal subsidy programs. In each case, the survey items focused on the underlying normative beliefs that act as guidelines for individual as well as collective responses. Analysis was primarily descriptive aimed at detailing both the range of these beliefs, and their dispersion across major population subgroups. Understanding the content and prevalence of these normative beliefs provides important information on the process of distributional change.

A majority of working respondents felt that individual actions such as asking for a pay increase or finding new employment, and collective responses such as union strikes and picketing, were sometimes the right response to wage inequity. A more substantial majority, however, felt that disruptive public protests and doing work poorly or incorrectly on purpose were never the right response. In each of the 1973 and 1974 surveys, three different types or dimensions of behavioral reactions to wage inequity emerged. Workers drew clear distinctions between reactions to wage inequity that involved lowering individual productivity and those that involved engaging in collective efforts to raise incomes. Furthermore, a distinction was made between the traditional forms of collective responses, such as union strikes, and those collective actions that were most often considered an illegitimate response to wage inequity. Of the three types of reactions, the least approved was action aimed at lessening individual productivity, followed by illegitimate collective actions, with the traditional approach receiving the most widespread endorsement.

Preferences for federal subsidy programs revealed that a majority of workers thought the government bore the primary responsibility for providing adequate health care to all citizens. Just one in five working respondents said the individual should be solely responsible for health care. But this strong support for the role of government subsidies was not similarly accorded to the housing and income subsidy programs. For the maintenance of material living standards, more workers favored placing primary responsibility on the individual rather than the government. Of the three programs, individual responsibility was most emphasized for maintaining an adequate job and standard of living.

Only small overall differences in beliefs both about labor market reactions and government intervention were found across major population subgroups. This, in part, indicates the pervasiveness and strength of these social norms themselves. Notwithstanding this widespread support, however, differences in these views were associated with socioeconomic position. The young and well educated more often found justification for the use of various tactics to redress wages, and were more likely to emphasize the role of the government in providing adequate material living standards. Preferences for federal subsidies were least likely to be held by upper-income families. Aside from the socioeconomic differences, individual circumstance, group affiliations, and social beliefs were associated with differences in these views. Female workers were less likely to endorse the use of wage redress tactics, but were somewhat more likely to favor federal job and income subsidies. Union membership and political party affiliation were also associated with differences in these views of the political economy, in the expected direction, although the differences were not as sharp or rigidly held as might have been expected.

Overall, these data indicate a widespread preference for maintaining material living standards by individual initiative rather than government subsidy. In addition, few workers found justification for the use of disruptive public protests or sabotage at the workplace in order to redress wage inequity. Yet, if long-term changes in these norms governing wage disputes and government subsidies follow generational lines, the preferences and views of the young and well-educated provide an indicator of the potential change. Among these subgroups, not only were alternate means for wage redress and income maintenance more attractive, but economic pressures among young households may also be relatively greater and so prompt change. The factors that motivate income redress through greater endorsement of workers' rights and government guarantees are investigated in the next chapter.

NOTES

1. Arthur M. Okun, *Equality and Efficiency: The Big Tradeoff* (Washington, D.C.: The Brookings Institution, 1975).

2. The factor model may be written, for the common-factor portion alone, as

$$Z = AF,$$

where Z represents the matrix of measurements on each of the survey items in standardized form, A is the matrix of common factor or pattern coefficients ("factor loadings"), and F is the matrix of measurements on each of the factors. The use of this technique involves replacing the units in the diagonal of the observed correlation matrix (R) with communalities for each variable. The communalities represent the proportion of common-factor variance for each of the survey questions; this procedure thus omits the unique determinants and their contributions to the error variance from the analysis model.

The initial estimates of communalities were the squared multiple correlations of each variable with the remaining set. The Kaiser criterion (the number of factors whose eigenvalues are greater than one) was used to determine the number of dimensions. The initial factor solution was followed by oblique rotation using Carroll's biquartimin method to allow for correlated factors. The transformation matrix (T) carries the factor pattern (A) to the oblique structure (S):

$$S = AT,$$

with the correlations among the factors given by

$$\phi = T'T.$$

See H. H. Harmon, *Modern Factor Analysis*, 2d ed. (Chicago: University of Chicago Press, 1967).

3. See Richard Musgrave, *The Theory of Public Finance* (New York: McGraw-Hill, 1959).

CHAPTER 8

SENSE OF INTERPERSONAL EQUITY: MOTIVATION FOR ACTION

It is the premise of this chapter that a heightened sense of income deprivation provides a significant motive for redress, and so instigates behavior aimed at distributional change. The research design ideally suited to test such behavioral propositions would first separate, under controlled conditions, the antecedent motive from the hypothesized consequent behavior, and, with independent observations on each, test their empirical relationship. In actuality, however, research designs often fall short of such causal modeling, substituting what some have termed "quasi-experimental" designs.[1]

Given the limitation imposed both by welfare methodology and cross-sectional survey techniques, this investigation also adopted an attenuated design: its attention is confined to testing the extent to which people's claims of deprivation were translated into behavioral predispositions directed toward increasing their distributional share; and correspondingly, for people who feel that they already receive more than they can justly claim, the extent to which they were favorably predisposed to a relative decline in their own income position.

Which modes of behavior will people choose to reduce their sense of income deprivation? Will workers choose to increase their inputs to gain a greater share, or will they try to exact a greater return from their employer for the same level of inputs, or from some other employer through job change? Or do people directly address their claims of income deprivation to the government for remedy, rather than turning to their employer?

Individual circumstance, including both the more objective aspects of people's economic position as well as their own views on the appropriateness and effectiveness of the various tactics, can be seen as deciding factors in the selection of a course of action to redress inequity. For example, among blue-collar workers the threat and use of organized work stoppages is often the most effective tactic, whereas individual wage bargaining and threats of job change are tactics more often used among white-collar workers, and especially so among the young. The poor, and those whose low relative economic position results from discriminatory practices, on the other hand, often advocate redress via government intervention.

Moreover, interlaced with these distinctions are the workers' own motives and beliefs, as not all would expect positive benefits to accrue to themselves personally from such tactics, nor would everyone think such income gains were justifiably won. In addition, while some constantly aspire to higher material living standards, others are more easily satiated, and still others give greater priority to the attainment of noneconomic goals, regardless of the perceived equitability of their income position.

ECONOMIC MOTIVATION

Before beginning this analysis, however, a review of the concept of motivation is in order.[2] The most widely known and used theory of economic motivation can be traced back to the English utilitarians. It holds that motivation is the product of "drive times habit." As this formulation implies, individual tastes and preferences can be considered constant, subsumed under the rubric of habit, if not held altogether exogenous to economic analysis. It is the "utility" of rewards that produces the motive drive; consequently, as the marginal utility of income varies with accomplishment, so does motivation. This basic formulation was later expanded and generalized to take into account both cross-cultural and cross-sectional differences in economic goals and aspirations.[3] The notion of drive was also expanded to encompass not only the impact of changing levels of income, but also the need for achievement as a more stable personality trait.[4] As a result, different levels of economic motivation were seen as ascribable to differences in economic need and aspiration, as well as to other more enduring cultural and personality factors.

More recent motivation theory has stressed a different basic model, the "value times expectancy" approach, which postulates motivation for economic gain to be the product of the strength of the expectancy that changes in one's own behavior will eventually lead to financial improvement, together with the value priority that is given to economic achievement.[5] Accordingly, motivation to engage in any particular behavior depends on whether these actions are instrumental for achieving a valued reward. Motivation, then, depends on both behavioral instrumentality and value priority; and variations in either will produce differences in motivation. But this distinction between drive and expectancy-based theories of motivation seems to be centered more on its conceptualization than on its affective components, since John Atkinson finds that each of these two theories leads to similar behavioral predictions in almost all situations.[6]

In this study the primary focus is on yet another theory, an exchange theory of motivation is based on the notion that a sense of inequity in interpersonal relations is in itself a motive for behavioral change.[7] Adams defines inequity as follows:

> Inequity exists for a person whenever he perceives that the ratio of his outcomes to inputs and the ratio of Others' outcomes to Others' inputs are unequal. This may happen either (a) when he and Other are in a direct exchange relationship or (b) when both are in an exchange relationship with a third party and the person compares himself to Others.[8]

Adams then goes on to postulate that the strength of the motivation to reduce inequity will be in proportion to the perceived magnitude of inequity.

What is of particular interest for this study is that this theory focuses directly on motivations stemming from interpersonal comparisons of distributive outcomes. Moreover, whereas both drive and expectancy theory almost always lead to the same behavioral predictions, an exchange theory of motivation often does not. The most crucial implication of this difference for the analysis of economic behavior is that while the former two theories "can be said to emphasize persons trying to maximize their positive outcomes, [exchange] theory emphasizes persons trying to balance their inputs against their outcomes."[9] In the first case, people are motivated toward ever higher incomes; in the second, people's motivations stem from notions of distributional balance. Nevertheless, it would be mistaken to consider the exchange theory as a competing motivational hypothesis; it stands rather as an added refinement. It is the granting of this additional source of economic motivation that allows for the possibility that less income may be preferred to more, even if your own income suffers relative decline; and, alternatively, that people may act to increase their income solely because others are now earning more. Furthermore, it is the recognition of the influence of both these sources of economic motivation that provides the dual motivational underpinning of the theoretical postulate outlined in Chapter 3. It was postulated there that increases in people's own (or others') income, when starting at low relative levels, also increase people's sense of well-being. However, a point is reached beyond which further additions to an already large income share only detract from, rather than adding to, perceived welfare. This point of transition, a position of maximum welfare, was then taken to represent underlying distributional preference; in the context of the exchange theory of motivation, it is this point of balance or income equity to which we are motivated.

MULTIVARIATE ANALYSIS OF BEHAVIORAL PREDISPOSITIONS

Does a heightened sense of interpersonal deprivation promote behavior aimed at income redress? Is the link between people's relative economic position and behavioral predispositions toward distributional change mediated to an important extent by the normative standards on which people base their perception of income equity or claims of deprivation? This chapter presents a multivariate model that sequentially examines (1) the separate influence of interpersonal wage comparisons and reported income satisfaction on behavioral predispositions aimed toward redress; (2) how measured income differences influence these predispositions toward distributional change, as well as income and expected price changes; and (3) estimates of the complete model, including both direct and indirect effects stemming from relative income position, standards used for comparison, socioeconomic characteristics, union membership, and political party identification.

Using this format, multiple regression estimates are presented for the correlates of expressed preferences for federal income, housing, and health care subsidies, as well as for predispositions to respond to wage inequity with a reduction in individual work effort, or to endorse collective reactions such as strikes or other less widely accepted tactics for redress. In doing so, this analysis integrates and extends the multivariate model first presented in Chapter 6. Figure 8.1 highlights the potential paths of influence of both objective and subjective sources of relative deprivation on these predispositions. This model explicitly recognizes that the underlying determinants of relative income evaluations may affect these behavioral predispositions directly, as well as indirectly through subjective income evaluations. Indeed, it is the significant net direct impact of subjective notions of income equity, apart from differences in objective conditions, that will indicate their importance.

PREFERENCES FOR FEDERAL SUBSIDY PROGRAMS

This section presents the results from a multivariate regression analysis of expressed preferences for government guarantees of income, housing, and health care programs. Table 8.1 displays the preferences for the income and job guarantee program as expressed in the 1973 and 1974 surveys; Table 8.2 examines housing and health care preferences as reported in the 1974 survey.

There were two important aspects to the analysis of these data. First, regression analysis focused on the multivariate correlates of preferences for each type of federal subsidy program. Here concern was focused on how the underlying determinants of income evaluations act to shape each of these policy

FIGURE 8.1

Multivariate Analysis Model of Behavioral Predispositions toward Distributional Change

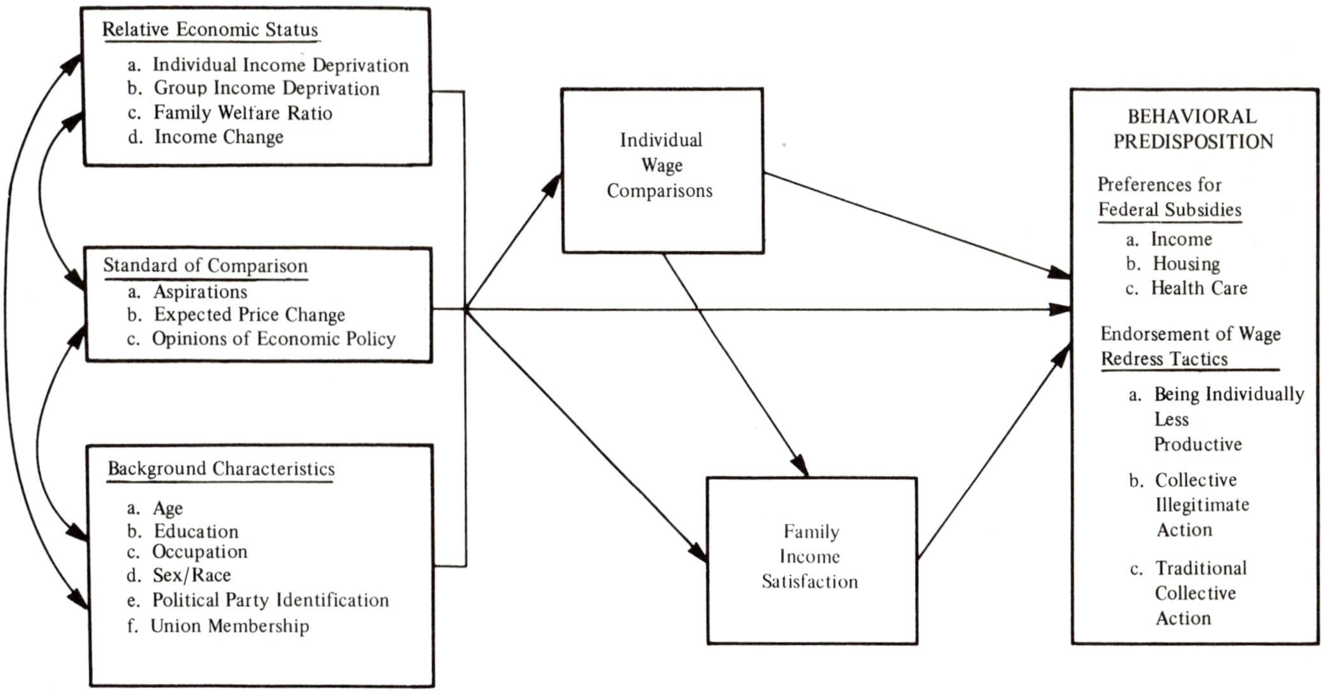

TABLE 8.1

Multiple Regression Analysis of Expressed Preferences for Federal Income Subsidies, 1973-74

Independent Variable	1973 (1)	1973 (2)	1973 (3)	1974 (1)	1974 (2)	1974 (3)
Wage comparisons	-.015	-.019	-.039	.034	.036	.042
	(0.40)	(0.51)	(1.07)	(0.95)	(1.02)	(1.23)
Income satisfaction	.176	.133	.100	.124	.064	.019
	(4.65)	(3.41)	(2.65)	(3.52)	(1.72)	(0.49)
Individual income deprivation		.102	.081		.067	.060
		(2.49)	(1.92)		(1.65)	(1.31)
Group income deprivation		.207	.131		.145	.125
		(5.29)	(2.62)		(3.97)	(2.51)
Family welfare ratio		-.046	-.041		.056	.044
		(1.03)	(0.92)		(1.27)	(0.96)
Income change		-.007	-.036		NA	NA
		(0.19)	(1.01)			
Expected price change		-.056	-.050		.036	.042
		(1.63)	(1.48)		(1.07	(1.29)
Aspirations (1 = high)			-.035			-.113
			(1.01)			(3.13)
Economic policy (1 = poor)			.089			.009
			(2.61)			(0.26)
Age (years)			.004			-.016
			(0.10)			(0.36)
Education (years)			.033			-.069
			(0.73)			(1.49)
Occupation (1 = blue-collar worker)			.044			.010
			(1.08)			(0.24)
Sex/race						
1 = male nonwhite			-.147			-.135
			(4.29)			(4.00)
1 = female white			-.016			-.020
			(0.38)			(0.47)
1 = female nonwhite			-.175			-.104
			(4.82)			(2.88)
Political party						
1 = Democrat			-.132			-.092
			(3.05)			(2.22)
1 = Republican			.072			.052
			(1.62)			(1.24)
Union						
1 = Union member			-.130			-.054
			(3.74)			(1.53)
Constant	2.77	3.13	3.23	2.90	3.06	3.93
SEE	1.43	1.40	1.33	1.25	1.23	1.19
RSQD (adjusted)	.026	.064	.160	.017	.049	.105

Note: Table entires are standardized partial beta coefficients, with associated t-statistics in parentheses. In all cases, a positive coefficient indicates that relatively low economic status as measured by the independent variables was associated with a more favorable attitude toward government guarantees. NA indicates variable not available in that survey year.

TABLE 8.2

Multiple Regression Analysis of Expressed Preferences for Federal Housing and Health Care Subsidies, 1974

Independent Variable	Health Care (1)	Health Care (2)	Health Care (3)	Housing (1)	Housing (2)	Housing (3)
Wage comparisons	.010	.016	.030	.007	.017	.015
	(0.27)	(0.44)	(0.84)	(0.21)	(0.49)	(0.44)
Income satisfaction	.107	.090	.064	.154	.119	.084
	(3.03)	(2.41)	(1.67)	(4.39)	(3.22)	(2.28)
Individual income deprivation		.013	.021		.039	.021
		(0.31)	(0.45)		(0.96)	(0.46)
Group income deprivation		.097	.141		.191	.152
		(2.62)	(2.78)		(5.26)	(3.10)
Family welfare ratio		-.016	-.016		-.028	-.052
		(0.35)	(0.35)		(0.64)	(1.15)
Expected price change		-.016	-.011		-.018	.037
		(0.48)	(0.34)		(0.55)	(1.15)
Aspirations (1 = high)			-.021			-.012
			(0.56)			(0.34)
Economic policy (1 = poor)			-.036			-.039
			(1.05)			(1.19)
Age (years)			-.031			.060
			(0.71)			(1.41)
Education (years)			-.154			-.066
			(3.28)			(1.46)
Occupation (1 = blue-collar worker)			.003			-.017
			(0.06)			(0.44)
Sex/race						
1 = male nonwhite			-.113			-.180
			(3.28)			(5.44)
1 = female white			.017			-.036
			(0.39)			(0.87)
1 = female nonwhite			-.087			-.231
			(2.37)			(6.48)
Political party						
1 = Democrat			-.051			-.062
			(1.20)			(1.51)
1 = Republican			.118			.039
			(2.75)			(0.94)
Union						
1 = Union member			-.046			-.010
			(1.28)			(0.28)
Constant	2.14	2.33	3.51	2.71	3.06	3.64
SEE	1.24	1.24	1.21	1.28	1.26	1.20
RSQD (adjusted)	.010	.014	.069	.022	.051	.136

Note: Table entires are standardized partial beta coefficients, with associated t-statistics in parentheses. In all cases, a positive coefficient indicates that relatively low economic status as measured by the independent variables was associated with a more favorable attitude toward government guarantees.

preferences. To the extent that these programs are distinct in their appeal, this will be relfected in differences in their underlying correlates. For the job and income guarantee program, analysis also examined the stability of the estimated relationships across independent cross-sectional samples.

The second major analytic goal was to investigate the more systematic sources and bases of preferences for income subsidies, apart from the specific program content. Although it was recognized that the specific content of federal programs will vary over time with changing circumstance, overall population predispositions toward nonmarket rather than market-based distribution represent a more enduring normative stance. Here concern was primarily focused on individual predictors and the stability of the estimated relationships across different policy types and survey dates.

Preferences for Job and Income Subsidies

Preferences for income and job guarantees by the federal government were not significantly related to people's own sense of interpersonal wage equity, but these voiced preferences were associated with reported satisfaction with income and standard of living (see equation 1, Table 8.1). Thus workers who were satisfied with their family income and living standard, no matter their sense of interpersonal wage equity, were significantly more likely to prefer having each individual "get ahead on their own" to having government subsidies. Based on just the influence of subjective income evaluations, these results suggest that income dissatisfaction, not interpersonal wage inequity, promotes redress through government intervention. Given that this subsidy program focused on both job and income standards, one would expect that a sense of income deprivation, either by interpersonal comparison or by one's own sense of dissatisfaction, would sway these voiced preferences. But these data indicate that people's perceptions of interpersonal wage equity did not affect what role they thought the government should play in the income allocation process. This lack of association, however, may only be superficial, resulting from counteracting factors: adoption of either policy extreme could enhance one's own sense of interpersonal equity, depending on relative economic circumstance and normative standards.

The importance of the role of subjective evaluations was further highlighted in the 1973 data. Even after taking account of actual income differences, reported satisfaction levels had a significant impact on these preferences. In the 1974 data, after taking account of actual income differences, the net impact of reported satisfaction was only marginal (see equation 2 in Table 8.1).

Earlier analysis has shown preferences for income subsidies to be heavily influenced by socioeconomic position and ideology. Consistent with this finding, estimated group income deprivation—constructed on the basis of what income differences exist between demographic subgroups and thus incorporating their indirect effects on preferences–demonstrated a significant and systematic impact on preferences. In each year, the higher the group's estimated mean income compared to the societal average, the less frequent support was voiced for federal job and income guarantees. Insofar as economic ideology or class stratification is responsive to differences in permanent incomes, this measure of group income deprivation forms the income analogue to economic ideology.

Although estimated group deprivation was itself an important predictor of income and standard of living satisfaction (but not of wage comparisons), each variable demonstrated an independent net effect on these expressed preferences in 1973. This indicates that the effect of group deprivation on preferences was not completely mediated by subjective assessments of income adequacy. It should be noted, however, that differences in family income, adjusted for family size and needs, were the most important predictor of reported satisfaction. While differences in the family welfare ratio variable did not correspond with differences in these policy preferences, their impact may be more indirect, and mediated by income satisfaction.

When the model incorporated differences in actual income position along with subjective evaluations, expressed preferences for federal income subsidies were more responsive to enduring differences in income position than to transitory changes in relative incomes. While preferences were associated with relatively permanent differences in subgroup incomes in both surveys, neither past income change nor expected price change demonstrated a significant impact on these income subsidy preferences in either year (see equation 2, Table 8.1).

When the full model was estimated, including differences in individual characteristics, standards of comparison, and group affiliations, the role of both the subjective and objective income variables remained unchanged (see equation 3 in Table 8.1). The estimated model indicates the importance of social and economic ideology on these policy preferences, apart from associated differences in relative income position. In each survey, self-identified Democrats were significantly more likely to endorse federal income and job guarantees. Republicans, on the other hand, were less likely to favor such programs, although the estimated difference was marginal in significance. In the 1973 survey, union members gave significantly greater support for federal income subsidies, but not in 1974. Nonwhites, both male and female, were significantly more likely to endorse federal subsidies. With regard to the impact of differences in standards of comparison on these policy preferences, high material aspirations were associated with preferences for an expanded role of the government, although only significantly so in the 1974 data. Interestingly, respondents who evaluated government economic policy as poor in 1973 preferred a greater reliance on the individual rather than expanded government intervention.

Preferences for Housing and Health Care Subsidies

In a fashion similar to preferences for job and income guarantees, reported income satisfaction, not interpersonal wage equity, was associated with housing and health care preferences (see equation 1 in Table 8.2). In each case, the higher the level of voiced satisfaction, the less the respondent favored government intervention. Conversely, those dissatisfied with their income were more likely to favor federal subsidies for housing and health care.

When the influences of actual income differences were included, income satisfaction remained a significant predictor, indicating its independent net direct effect on these subsidy preferences (see equation 2 in Table 8.2). Of the various measures of relative income position, only group income deprivation demonstrated a direct and systematic influence on preferences for housing and health care programs. These data thus again indicate that although income satisfaction has important independent effects on policy preferences, actual income differences are not completely mediated by subjective income evaluations. In particular, relatively enduring differences in subgroup incomes had a strong direct impact on these policy preferences.

The complete model, including differences in socioeconomic characteristics, showed housing and health care subsidy preferences to be laregly unaffected by differences in age, occupation, and expected consumer price changes (see equation 3 in Table 8.2). Nonwhites were significantly more likely to favor government intervention, perhaps reflecting the current availability of adequate housing and health care in their communities. Aside from this somewhat greater support from nonwhites, only the variables that represented group income deprivation and subjective income satisfaction mattered for housing subsidy preferences. For health care programs, the higher the educational attainment of the respondents, the more likely they were to also favor an expanded role of the federal government in providing health care. The impact of political affiliation and union membership was minimal, as only self-identified Republicans were significantly less likely to favor government provisions of health care services, but not of housing.

Systematic Influences on Subsidy Preferences

The overall findings concerning preferences for federal subsidy programs are summarized in Figure 8.2. As before, this model interposed subjective income evaluations between relative income position and other socioeconomic and background characteristics, and behavioral predispositions aimed toward distributional change. In this figure, the narrower solid arrows denote the major systematic paths of influence of relative income position on income evaluations as documented in previous chapters. The wider solid arrows reflect the

FIGURE 8.2

Summary Display of the Determinants of Preferences
for Federal Subsidies

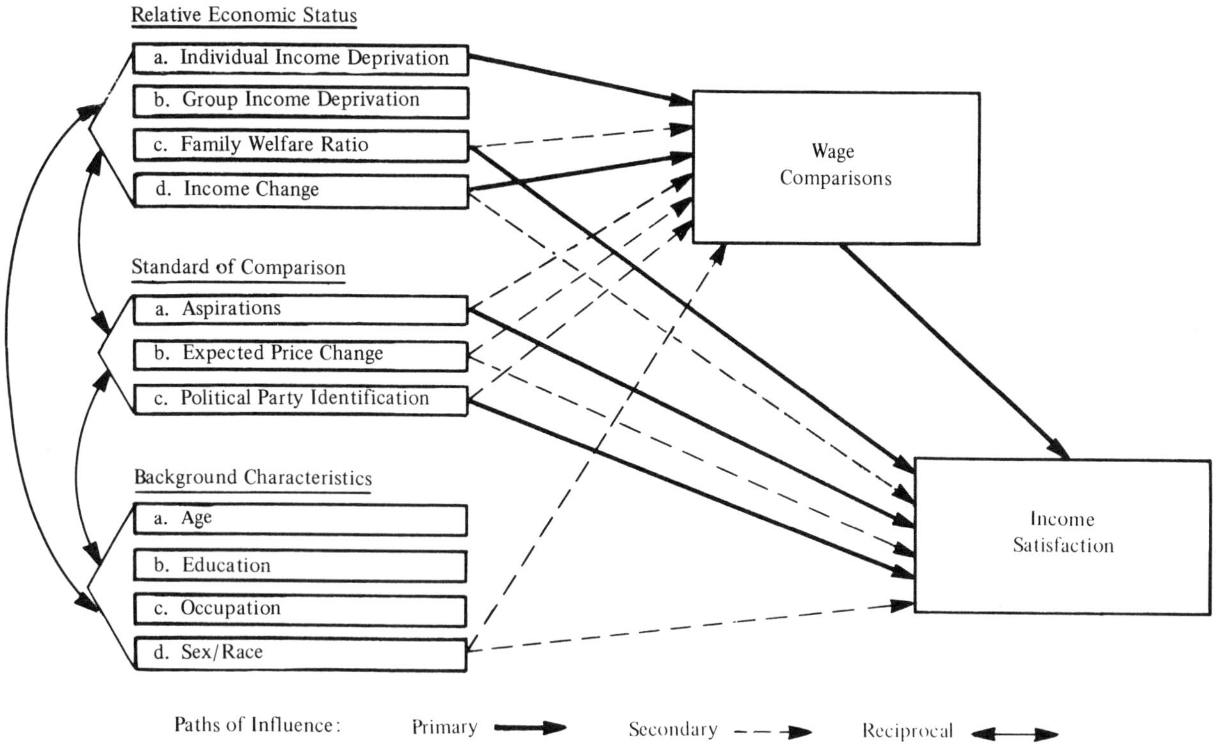

significant and systematic direct links uncovered in the preceding analysis. The dashed arrows indicate that for some of the subsidy programs, or in one but not both surveys, a particular variable demonstrated a significant association with policy preferences.

An inspection of this chart suggests that differences in relative income position and subjective evaluations affect these behavioral predispositions in characteristically different ways. Of the four measures of relative income position, only group income deprivation directly affected these preferences for government subsidies, yet this same variable did not show any other significant link to subjective income evaluations. In contrast, individual income deprivation, family welfare ratio, and past income change, although each demonstrated a significant and systematic impact on subjective income evaluations, had no direct effect on these policy preferences. The impact on preferences from these other sources of income deprivation was mediated by perceptions of interpersonal wage equity, and in turn, by income satisfaction.

These results suggest that only relatively permanent differences in relative income position were directly associated with preferences for expanded federal subsidies. Transitory differences in wage incomes, as well as the ability of current incomes to meet current family needs, were translated into predispositions toward federal subsidies only insofar as they first affected overall income satisfaction. Ultimately this serves to mute the impact of these transitory changes on policy preferences, because changes in satisfaction depend not only on actual changes in accomplishment, but also on changes in expectations and aspirations. Since overall satisfaction readings remained remarkably stable over the 1974-75 recession period, the responsiveness of aspirations and expectations to changes in the economic environment cannot be discounted.

Other, less systematic, influences on these policy preferences stem from differences in education, material aspirations, political identification, and union affiliation. In part, the lack of systematic impact was due to the specific content of the various programs, and in part because of changing political and economic circumstances between the two survey dates. More generally, these results indicate that federal subsidy programs are more apt to be affected by changing views and opinions among population subgroups, as represented by education, group identification, and evaluations of current economic policy.

ENDORSEMENT OF WAGE REDRESS TACTICS

This analysis is concerned with the underlying determinants of people's willingness to endorse actions that broaden their range of options when seeking wage redress. Three distinct dimensions of labor market reactions to wage inequity, representing predispositions toward being individually less productive and toward the use of illegitimate and traditional collective actions, were exam-

TABLE 8.3

Multiple Regression Analysis of Predispositions toward Being Individually Less Productive to Redress Wage Inequity

Independent Variable	1973 (1)	1973 (2)	1973 (3)	1974 (1)	1974 (2)	1974 (3)
Wage comparisons	-.037	-.049	-.054	-.044	-.046	-.037
	(0.96)	(1.28)	(1.40)	(1.24)	(1.29)	(1.07)
Income satisfaction	.111	.068	.042	.112	.071	.064
	(2.92)	(1.72)	(1.05)	(3.17)	(1.91)	(1.68)
Individual income deprivation		.045	.102		.069	.124
		(1.08)	(2.25)		(1.67)	(2.70)
Group income deprivation		.130	.174		.101	.072
		(3.24)	(3.27)		(2.73)	(1.43)
Family welfare ratio		.046	.005		.026	-.041
		(1.02)	(0.11)		(0.58)	(0.87)
Income change		.092	.103		NA	NA
		(2.53)	(2.71)			
Expected price change		.003	.006		.065	.066
		(0.09)	(0.16)		(1.95)	(2.00)
Aspirations (1 = high)			.032			-.036
			(0.88)			(0.98)
Economic policy (1 = poor)			.037			.040
			(1.03)			(1.19)
Age (years)			.007			.122
			(0.16)			(2.77)
Education (years)			-.017			-.058
			(0.36)			(1.24)
Occupation (1 = blue-collar worker)			-.042			-.054
			(0.95)			(1.33)
Sex/race						
1 = male nonwhite			-.067			-.122
			(1.85)			(3.56)
1 = female white			.150			.085
			(3.50)			(2.02)
1 = female nonwhite			.051			-.007
			(1.32)			(0.18)
Political party						
1 = Democrat			.006			-.031
			(0.13)			(0.74)
1 = Republican			.086			.016
			(1.81)			(0.37)
Union						
1 = Union member			.018			-.055
			(0.49)			(1.54)
Constant	-0.20	-0.32	-0.40	-0.13	-0.64	-0.52
SEE	0.85	0.83	0.82	0.82	0.81	0.79
RSQD (adjusted)	.008	.029	.053	.009	.026	.074

Note: Table entires are standardized partial beta coefficients, with associated t-statistics in parentheses. In all cases, a positive coefficient indicates that low relative economic status as measured by the independent variables was associated with a greater willingness to endorse being less productive and engage in collective actions to redress wage inequity. NA indicates variable not available in that survey year.

ined. Each dimension was analyzed both for the individual correlates of each particular type of reaction, and for the systematic patterns of association that determine overall predispositions toward wage redress. For each behavioral reaction, regression estimates are listed sequentially in order to highlight the significant paths in the hypothesized model (see Figure 8.1), and replicated in each of the 1973 and 1974 survey samples. Respondents' scores on each reaction dimension were estimated on the basis of a factor analysis, with negative values indicating greater relative approval of the use of a particular tactic, and positive deviations indicating that more often a tactic was judged "never right."

Redress through Lowered Productivity

The simple association between subjective income evaluations and approval of lowering individual productivity revealed that these predispositions were not responsive to perceptions of interpersonal wage equity. In contrast, voiced income satisfaction demonstrated a significant association with this productivity dimension (see equation 1 in Table 8.3). In each sample analyzed, the higher the level of reported income satisfaction, the less willing workers were to approve of being individually less productive to redress wage inequity.

Once the underlying differences in relative income position were taken into account, the net direct association of income satisfaction with approval of lowering productivity was insignificant (see equation 2 in Table 8.3). This indicates that subjective income evaluations, apart from the identifiable role accounted for by differences in actual income position, had no independent effect on this predisposition. Although subjective income assessments did not directly affect predispositions toward lowering productivity, the respondents' relative income position, on which these evaluations are based, did demonstrate a significant direct impact. In each survey, individual income deprivation was significantly associated with lowering productivity in response to wage inequity. This indicates that workers whose earnings were below what other workers with similar skills received, were more likely to endorse being individually less productive (see equation 3 in Table 8.3). In addition, the amount of their last income change affected these predispositions toward being individually less productive (1973 data). The larger the last income change, the less likely people were to endorse being less productive. It is tempting to interpret this increased predisposition toward being individually less productive as a hostile reaction to what was considered a less than adequate pay raise. And because this reaction was tied to the most recent wage change, this hostility may be only temporary, easily reversed with future wage increases.

This view is supported by the more consistent correspondence of the reaction of lessening work effort with income differences as compared to other similar workers, rather than with more stable differences in subgroup incomes.

Because these reactions were concerned more with the transitory rather than permanent aspects of relative income position, being individually less productive can be interpreted as a response to immediate surroundings, and to what progress has been recently made. And because these reactions were dominated by transitory changes in income, this indicates that low productivity is a response to changing income levels, rather than a feature of a low and stable income position.

The third equation in each set estimated the full model, including the influence of individual circumstance as reflected by demographic characteristics, political affiliations, and union membership. As documented previously, hardly anyone said that being individually less productive was justifiable at any time. This analysis reaffirmed that finding by demonstrating its lack of association with differences in aspirations, age, education, occupation, political affiliations, and union membership; the one consistent exception being white females, who were, compared to white males, significantly less likely to endorse being individually less productive to redress wage inequity.

Redress Through Collective Actions

The simple association of subjective income assessments and predispositions toward the use of collective actions—illegitimate and traditional—was significant for each type of action orientation, and in each sample analyzed (see equation 1 in Tables 8.4-8.5). In each case, the use of collective action to redress inequity found greater approval among those who were dissatisfied with their income. As with predispositions toward lowering productivity, reported levels of income satisfaction, rather than interpersonal wage comparisons, were significantly associated with these behavioral predispositions. Consequently, the more satisfied a worker was with his income and standard of living, the less likely he was to endorse action to redress wage inequity, no matter the means, nor the sense of interpersonal equity.

The second regression equation in each analysis set included the influence of the underlying differences in relative income position. In contrast to predispositions toward being individually less productive, subjective income evaluations demonstrated a net direct impact on these predispositions toward collective action (see equation 2 in Tables 8.4-8.5). Consequently, the greater the current satisfaction with income and standard of living, the less people were predisposed to endorse collective action, apart from the influence of actual income differences. Because both objective and subjective sources of deprivation had independent effects, these results indicate that differences in actual income position are not completely mediated by income satisfaction, nor are differences in the influence of income satisfaction on these reactions completely accounted for by actual income differences.

TABLE 8.4

Multiple Regression Analysis of Predispositions toward the Use of Illegitimate Collective Action to Redress Wage Inequity

Independent Variable	1973 (1)	1973 (2)	1973 (3)	1974 (1)	1974 (2)	1974 (3)
Wage comparisons	.035	.049	.036	-.035	-.031	-.019
	(0.91)	(1.27)	(0.98)	(1.01)	(0.90)	(0.57)
Income satisfaction	.107	.141	.095	.207	.055	.138
	(2.81)	(3.58)	(2.49)	(5.92)	(4.25)	(3.74)
Individual income deprivation		-.106	-.058		.075	.116
		(2.57)	(1.35)		(1.85)	(2.60)
Group income deprivation		-.035	.060		.176	.145
		(0.87)	(1.18)		(4.88)	(2.97)
Family welfare ratio		-.047	-.033		.004	-.043
		(1.05)	(0.74)		(0.10)	(0.96)
Income change		-.066	-.038		NA	NA
		(1.81)	(1.04)			
Expected price change		-.087	-.027		.007	.015
		(2.49)	(0.82)		(0.20)	(0.46)
Aspirations (1 = high)			.128			-.033
			(3.70)			(0.93)
Economic policy (1 = poor)			-.109			-.003
			(3.17)			(0.09)
Age (years)			.077			.084
			(1.80)			(1.98)
Education (years)			-.212			-.117
			(4.67)			(2.59)
Occupation (1 = blue-collar worker)			.059			-.113
Sex/race						
1 = male nonwhite			-.033			-.097
			(0.95)			(2.92)
1 = female white			.119			.038
			(2.91)			(0.92)
1 = female nonwhite			.042			-.011
			(1.15)			(0.32)
Political party						
1 = Democrat			-.042			-.066
			(0.96)			(1.61)
1 = Republican			.060			.050
			(1.32)			(1.20)
Union						
1 = Union member			-.066			-.116
			(1.87)			(3.38)
Constant	-0.23	-0.67	0.19	-0.31	-0.13	0.32
SEE	0.81	0.80	0.75	0.80	0.78	0.75
RSQD (adjusted)	.013	.036	.147	.037	.069	.137

Note: Table entires are standardized partial beta coefficients, with associated t-statistics in parentheses. In all cases, a positive coefficient indicates that low relative economic status as measured by the independent variables was associated with a greater willingness to engage in illegitimate collective actions to redress wage inequity. NA indicates variable not available in that survey year.

TABLE 8.5

Multiple Regression Analysis of Predispositions toward the Use of Traditional Collective Action to Redress Wage Inequity

Independent Variable	1973 (1)	1973 (2)	1973 (3)	1974 (1)	1974 (2)	1974 (3)
Wage comparisons	.027	.030	.019	-.066	-.052	-.032
	(0.72)	(0.78)	(0.53)	(1.87)	(1.44)	(0.97)
Income satisfaction	.148	.118	.084	.098	.105	.092
	(3.90)	(3.01)	(2.21)	(2.75)	(2.80)	(2.55)
Individual income deprivation		-.041	.042		-.064	.035
		(0.99)	(0.98)		(1.53)	(0.81)
Group income deprivation		.122	.130		.067	.161
		(3.06)	(2.59)		(1.80)	(3.36)
Family welfare ratio		.038	-.003		-.022	-.056
		(0.83)	(0.07)		(0.50)	(1.27)
Income change		.003	-.004		NA	NA
		(0.07)	(0.10)			
Expected price change		-.055	-.020		-.021	-.018
		(1.57)	(0.60)		(0.61)	(0.56)
Aspirations (1 = high)			.073			-.011
			(2.12)			(0.31)
Economic policy (1 = poor)			-.025			-.097
			(0.71)			(3.03)
Age (years)			.127			.093
			(2.98)			(2.24)
Education (years)			-.086			-.282
			(1.91)			(6.35)
Occupation (1 = blue-collar worker)			-.004			-.031
			(0.10)			(0.82)
Sex/race						
1 = male nonwhite			-.002			-.081
			(0.05)			(2.50)
1 = female white			.166			.154
			(4.07)			(3.84)
1 = female nonwhite			.010			.038
			(0.29)			(1.08)
Political party						
1 = Democrat			-.030			-.118
			(0.68)			(2.95)
1 = Republican			.124			.031
			(2.78)			(0.75)
Union						
1 = Union member			-.201			-.140
			(5.74)			(4.15)
Constant	-0.35	-0.30	-0.36	-0.73	0.20	1.09
SEE	0.81	0.81	0.76	0.85	0.84	0.77
RSQD (adjusted)	.023	.039	.153	.008	.012	.172

Note: Table entries are standardized partial beta coefficients, with associated t-statistic. in parentheses. In all cases, a positive coefficient indicates that low relative economic status as measured by the independent variables was associated with a greater willingness to engage in traditional collective actions to redress wage inequity. NA indicates variable not available in that survey year.

The most important objective source shaping collective predispositions was estimated group income deprivation (see equation 3 in Tables 8.4-8.5). For both illegitimate and traditional collective actions, respondents with lower expected incomes, as based on differences in skills and abilities, were significantly more likely to endorse their use. The only exception was with regard to the dimension of illegitimate collective action in the 1973 survey. Thus predispositions toward collective actions were dependent in part on both current income satisfaction and the more permanent differences in relative income position. These collective orientations were also less subject to the influences of transitory income change, in comparison to predispositions toward lowering productivity.

Estimates of the full model indicate the important and direct influence of differences in socioeconomic and other background characteristics on reported approval of collective actions. For predispositions toward illegitimate collective actions, higher educational attainment was associated with greater approval of their use. In contrast to the systematic association with education, differences in age, sex, race, and occupation showed less systematic influence on predispositions toward illegitimate collective action (see equation 3 in Tables 8.4-8.5).

Predispositions toward the use of traditional collective actions demonstrated a greater association with socioeconomic characteristics than did either of the other two orientations. Both the young and well educated were more likely to endorse these traditional responses to wage inequity. Although blue-collar workers were not significantly more likely to endorse these traditional collective actions, union members reported significantly greater approval. In 1974, blue-collar workers as well as union members were also somewhat more likely to endorse illegitimate collective actions. That these traditional reactions fall more along familiar ideological lines was attested by their significant association with political party affiliation. In 1973, self-identified Republicans were more likely to disapprove of the use of traditional collective actions, and in 1974, self-identified Democrats more willingly endorsed the use of traditional collective actions. In contrast, approval of illegitimate collective action was not associated with political party identification (see equation 3 in Table 8.5).

The collective action orientations demonstrated some responsiveness to differences in evaluations of government economic policy. Respondents who felt the government was doing a poor job with regard to aggregate problems of inflation and unemployment were more likely to endorse illegitimate collective actions in 1973, and traditional collective actions in 1974. In each case, the less confidence people had in the government's ability to control inflation and unemployment, the more willingly they endorsed collective action to redress inequitable wages. The lack of a consistent association across time between economic policy evaluations and these labor market reactions may indicate either the changing focus of the relationship in response to changing conditions, or that the relationship itself was by in large weak or nonexistent.

High income aspirations (1973 data) did correspond with more frequent endorsement of collective action, although respondents who reported high material aspirations in 1974 did not voice greater approval. Respondents with high aspirations for real income improvements were especially more likely to endorse tactics more widely considered illegitimate. Although the young were both more likely to voice approval of these so-called illegitimate actions and were also more apt to express aspirations for future income increases, this association between income aspirations and willingness to endorse collective action was maintained even after age differences were controlled (see equation 3 in Tables 8.4–8.5).

Interestingly, on each type of behavioral reaction to wage inequity, white females were significantly less likely to approve of its use compared to white males. This was true with regard to collective responses to wage inequity as well as to lessening individual productivity. In contrast, nonwhite respondents—male or female—did not show any systematic differences in the extent of their support for these various tactics, although they were significantly more likely to voice subjective income deprivation. This may indicate either that women are less attracted to collective or individual confrontations with employers, or that because of the types of occupations they hold, such actions offer less promise for redress. For example, the relatively lower support found among women for traditional collective actions may in part reflect the greater proportions of women employed in occupations thus far resistant to unionization.

Summary of Predispositions toward Wage Redress

These above analyses are summarized in Figure 8.3. As before, the narrower solid arrows indicate the major relationships between socioeconomic position and subjective income evaluations as documented in previous chapters; the broader solid arrows indicate that systematic relationships were documented between these variables and predispositions toward wage redress, across action types and survey dates; the dashed arrows represent a significant association either for one particular type of labor market reaction or for a relationship that failed to be replicated. The following is a summary of these results.

Subjective income evaluations, apart from any associated differences in actual income position, had an independent and direct effect on the approval accorded these various wage redress tactics. Although justification for being individually less productive did not vary directly with subjective income evaluations, this association was consistently found for predispositions toward both illegitimate and traditional collective actions. Heightened predispositions toward the use of collective actions to gain wage redress were associated with dissatisfaction with income and standard of living, not with unfavorable interpersonal wage comparisons. Although the wage comparison measures were conceptually

FIGURE 8.3

Summary Display of the Determinants of Endorsement of Wage Redress Tactics

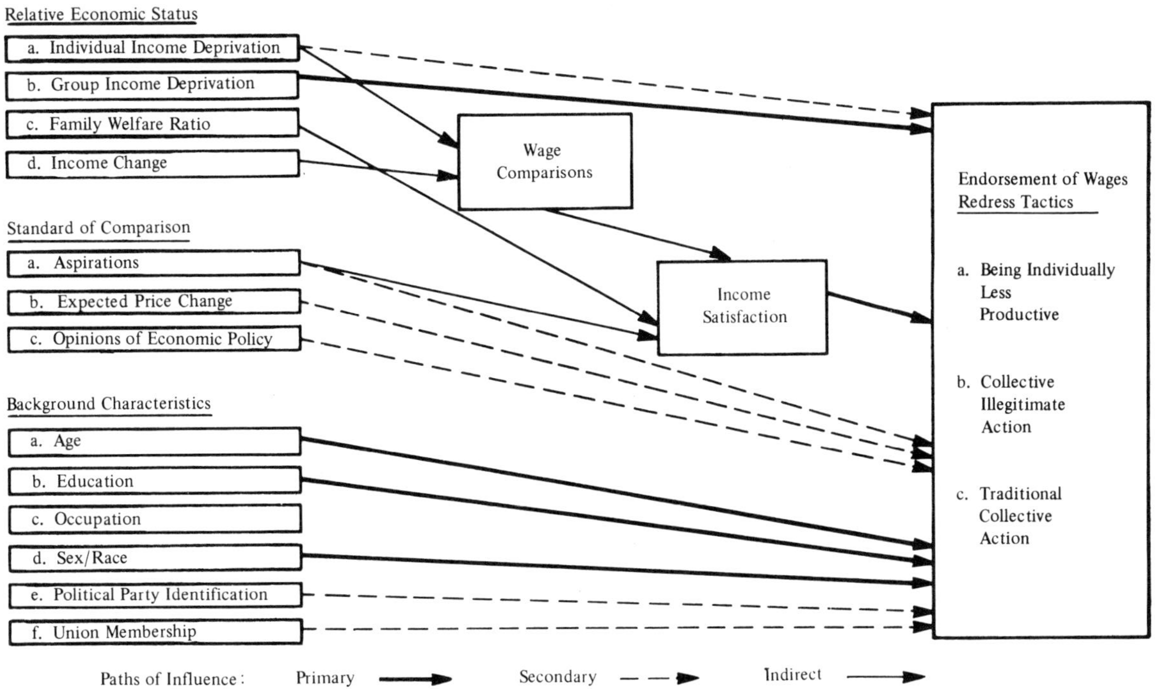

closer to these labor market orientations, these data suggest that dispositions toward collective actions were responsive to a broader, more inclusive notion of economic well-being. However, interpersonal wage evaluations could have had an indirect effect on these behavioral orientations, since wage comparisons were found to be an important determinant of overall income satisfaction. In addition, income satisfaction mediates not only perceptions of interpersonal wage equity, but also the adequacy of family income, past wage increases, and aspirations (see Figure 8.3).

Being individually less productive was more often condoned by workers whose own level of income was less than that of others with similar skills and abilities. In this manner, individual income differences rather than overall relative income position affected approval of lower productivity. Thus, reduction in work effort was as likely to have found justification by workers at all income levels, but more so if the individual worker was paid less than other comparable workers. In addition, the size of the worker's last income change affected willingness to justify reductions in productivity. Reacting to wage inequity by a reduction in work effort was thus more responsive to the worker's changing individual circumstance. In contrast, collective action orientations were associated more with enduring differences in relative income position, lower income subgroups being more likely to approve of the use of collective actions to redress inequity. This was not a matter of adequate income to meet family needs, but simply a matter of relative income position.

Interestingly, neither past income change nor expected price change was significantly associated with collective action orientations. This suggests that any impact from these sources could only be indirect, via income satisfaction. It should be noted, however, that unmet income aspirations did directly prompt a greater endorsement of collective tactics in the 1973 survey, and respondents who felt the government was doing a poor job in managing economic policy in 1974 were also more likely to endorse collective responses. In all, these transitory changes in relative income position, as well as the concurrent changes in the performance of the aggregate economy, demonstrated little direct and systematic impact on predispositions toward collective action. Rather, these transitory sources of deprivation were mediated by subjective income assessments. Nonetheless, these sources of deprivation did demonstrate the ability to generalize about labor market reactions in some instances in the past, and can be expected to do so again.

Overall, orientations toward these labor market reactions demonstrated a strong correspondence to both economic and social position. The young and well-educated workers were more likely to endorse wage redress through collective actions. Greater acceptance was found among the young for the more traditional actions, and among the well educated for the more illegitimate collective actions. In the one case, the passage of time promotes greater acceptance of current practices; in the other, attitudes toward the currently less acceptable often find favor among the educated, those best adapted to socioeconomic change.

NOTES

1. Donald T. Campbell and Julian C. Stanely, *Experimental and Quasi-Experimental Designs for Research* (Chicago: Rand McNally, 1966).

2. On this topic, see Edward E. Lawler, *Pay and Organizational Effectiveness* (New York: McGraw-Hill, 1971), chap. 5.

3. See, for example, George Katona, Burkhard Strumpel, and Ernest Zahn, *Aspirations and Affluence: Comparative Studies in the United States and Western Europe* (New York: McGraw-Hill, 1971).

4. John W. Atkinson, *An Introduction to Motivation* (Princeton: Van Nostrand, 1964).

5. See, for example, Gerald Gurin and Patricia Gurin, "Expectancy Theory in the Study of Poverty," *Journal of Social Issues* 26 (Spring 1970): 83-104; and Richard T. Curtin, "Well-Being, Goals, and Motivation for Economic Advancement," in *Economic Means for Human Needs*, ed. Burkhard Strumpel (Ann Arbor: Institute for Social Research, University of Michigan, 1976).

6. Atkinson, op. cit.

7. J. Stacy Adams, "Wage Inequities, Productivity, and Work Quality," *Industrial Relations* 3 (October 1963): 9-16; J. Stacy Adams, "Toward an Understanding of Inequity," *Journal of Abnormal and Social Psychology* 67 (November 1963): 422-36; and J. Stacy Adams, "Injustice in Social Exchange," in *Advances in Experimental Psychology*, vol. 2, ed. L. Berkowitz (New York: Academic Press, 1965).

8. Adams, "Injustice in Social Exchange," op. cit., p. 280.

9. Edward E. Lawler, "Equity Theory as a Predictor of Productivity and Work Quality," *Psychological Bulletin* 70 (December 1968): 598.

CHAPTER

9

PARAGONS AND PARADIGMS OF DISTRIBUTIONAL CHANGE

GOALS OF ANALYSIS: A RECAPITULATION

Every society is faced with the task of allocating scarce and valued economic resources among its members. Public policy cannot be neutral in this regard, for even if programs were designed to leave the existing distribution unchanged, these policies nonetheless express a distinct normative standard of economic justice. How income is distributed is also a matter of economic importance, since to accept some particular distribution as equitable is to also accept the consequences of such a distribution on production, employment, and societal integration.

This interdependence of distributional equity and productive efficiency forms one of the most central economic choices open to society. Yet when seeking a resolution, public policy discussion all too often rests on a simplified and static comparison of the actual to the ideal. Current income shares, for example, are often compared to the egalitarian ideal of equality. Transition from the real to the ideal is, however, nowhere discussed, leaving only paragons of distributional justice instead of behavioral paradigms that could offer practical policy guidance.

An understanding of the systematic links between the current income distribution, sensed interpersonal equity or deprivation, and consequent behavior aimed at distributional redress is important for making informed judgments on the distributional impact of alternate economic policies. As the effective use of fiscal and monetary policy must be based on knowledge of the underlying behavioral parameters, so too does distribution policy. Spending and tax programs, interest rate and money supply policies, each rely in part on the responses of behavioral units to accomplish their ultimate aims. Propensities to spend and save are crucial elements in their overall design. And such behavioral papameters are viewed both as individual phenomena and as representing collective outcomes. Not so with distribution policy. Here economic analysis models have yet to directly incorporate such behavioral parameters. The implicit assumption is that the relationships between economic magnitudes and their changes over time are left unaltered by preferences for and evaluations of people's own relative income position.

The exclusion of distributional equity as a concern of positive economic analysis has often been advocated because scientific analysis cannot objectively resolve distributional problems. This is so because interpersonal equity refers to a human experience unique to the moment, to the circumstance, and to the person. And even if distributional preferences could be known fully and with certainty, there is no scientific methodology on which to base their aggregation. Given these severe limitations, distributional ideals, it is argued, must suffice as guidelines for policy.

The principal purpose of this study was to make a contribution to our understanding of how interpersonal income comparisons affect economic choice. In particular, this investigation has focused on what criteria people use for judging the equitability of their share of income, and how these perceptions of distributional equity in turn affect economic behavior. The analytic framework did not, in any way, draw on a normative theory of income distribution. Rather, it was intended to provide a descriptive outline of the effects of interpersonal income comparisons on the well-being of individuals and on behavioral choice. While differences in income comparison standards rest on value judgments, propositions not capable of refutation by empirical analysis, they are nonetheless descriptive of how people evaluate their share of income in relation to others. Empirical analysis can therefore seek to sort out the relative impacts of various evaluative criteria on people's sense of distributional equity and on predispositions toward distributional change. The simple recognition that normative judgments must be made separate and distinct from positive economic analysis does not preclude the empirical investigation and analysis of interpersonal income comparisons.

The research design utilized personal interview surveys to ascertain both relative income evaluations and behavioral predispositions. Although questionnaire items can in no sense measure individual well-being, they can help to determine which criteria people use in making their evaluations, and whether these income evaluations in turn affect behavioral predispositions. The major dimensions of people's sense of interpersonal equity, the bases of these perceptions, and their consequences are detailed below in summary fashion.

PERCEPTIONS OF INCOME EQUITY

One out of every two workers, in three independent representative samples of working Americans conducted between 1973 and 1975, felt that they received less pay than they deserved in comparison to other workers. In contrast, when asked to rate how satisfactory they found their household's standard of living, only one in ten working respondents rated themselves dissatisfied during this same period. The widespread satisfaction with material living levels attests the ability of available economic resources to meet current consumption standards. Yet, based on standards of interpersonal equity, how these resources were distributed found much less acceptance. These differences in evaluations thus point to the difference between income adequacy and income equity, as what was often reported as satisfactory was nonetheless held as inequitably low by comparative standards.

The period covered by these surveys contained the sharpest and deepest postwar recession. Yet, subjective income evaluations remained remarkably stable over this period, if not marginally improved by late 1975 over the November 1973 reading. Although both interpersonal wage comparisons and income and standard of living satisfaction exhibited this upward drift, no significant trend in income evaluations was evidenced by these data. This overall stability in subjective evaluations, in the face of economic adversity, indicates that the criteria on which these evaluations were based shifted along with changing economic circumstances. Although many individuals may have changed in a favorable as well as unfavorable direction, the aggregate declines in income and employment, as well as rapid price increases, were not directly translated into lessened overall levels of felt well-being.

Analysis demonstrated that receiving less pay than workers felt they deserved was associated with a heightened sense of income dissatisfaction, but the converse was not true. Those who felt they were paid more than they deserve in comparison to other workers did not report greater income satisfaction than those who reported being paid equitably. Although wage comparisons did affect income satisfaction in this nonsymmetrical manner, interpersonal wage comparisons did not directly affect satisfaction with material living standards; evaluations of relative wages only indirectly affected people's appraisals of their overall living standards through income satisfaction. Importantly, this structure of income evaluations was replicated in each of the survey samples.

The response patterns for these subjective income evaluations also indicated a decreasing sense of deprivation as the basis of evaluations was broadened from individual wage comparisons to household living standards. Thus while interpersonal wage deprivation was much more prevalent than dissatisfaction with living standards, this sense of deprivation was much more limited in its scope, and only partially and indirectly translated into a lessened sense of overall economic well-being. But this is not to say that wage comparisons lack behavioral consequence. Nor does it diminish their importance. But insofar as widespread satisfaction with levels of material living are able to neutralize critical evaluations of relative earnings position, this will blunt issues of distributional equity, and temper discontent.

These self-reported income evaluations, since they are descriptive of people's own assessments of well-being, can serve as important indicators of changes in economic welfare. The detailed data presented on income evaluations of major groups of U.S. workers serves to inventory differences in perceptions of well-being, and provide a partial assessment of the effects of socioeconomic position on individual welfare. As social indicators of well-being or discontent, these data form benchmarks to gauge subsequent change, especially differential change among population subgroups. Few significant differences were found among major population groups, aside from income subgroups, in any one survey; and over the 1973-75 period, no systematic trends among particular population subgroups were evidenced. Of course, since changes in relative income position are not quickly or easily accomplished, the stability of these evaluations over this three-year period was not unexpected.

BASES OF INCOME COMPARISONS

Most people did not believe unequal incomes to be inherently unjust, or that incomes should be necessarily equal. Most accepted the notion that those who contribute a greater share of inputs should be accorded a greater share of outputs. When questioned in 1973, three in every four workers felt that such things as skill, ability, and effort made on the job should count more in determining wages. Nonperformance related criteria, such as education and seniority, were seen as less important for the determination of a fair wage.

Multivariate analysis revealed that only differences between current income and referent or expected income, based on broadly defined demographic and skill classifications, were associated with interpersonal wage comparisons. Workers who earned less than others with similar skills more frequently voiced deprivation, regardless of their level of income. But low wages as such were not a significant source of interpersonal deprivation. What differences existed between income reference groups were discounted when making wage comparisons. These results indicate that enduring differences in relative income position, such as between socioeconomic classes, did not contribute to people's sense of interpersonal equity or deprivation. Rather, these income differentials were widely accepted as legitimate.

People's evaluations of their overall living standard were more egalitarian. These self-ratings were dependent on the relative level of household income, adjusted for family size and needs. They were thus more concerned with relative consumption than income position. Here equal rather than proportional income shares formed the basis of comparative evaluations.

This difference in the basis of income evaluations parallels the distinction between the size distribution among income classes and the functional distribution of income. The application of these interrelated standards of distributional justice served both to motivate the equalization of the size distribution and, at the same time, to justify maintaining sufficient income differentials to insure economic efficiency. In this manner, relative income evaluations reflected the preferred trade-off between these competing goals.

Whether one standard of distributional justice is advocated over another is not just a matter of normative choice, but also of individual circumstance. Income aspirations as well as past and expected income change demonstrated important relationships with current income evaluations. Income change had its primary influence on interpersonal wage comparisons, while high material aspirations led directly to lessened overall satisfaction. In addition, people's own sense of dissatisfaction was either eased or exacerbated by the confidence they had in the economic policies of the federal government to combat the twin problems of inflation and unemployment.

It is important to stress that each of the major sources of interpersonal wage deprivation involved what may be termed transitory fluctuations in relative economic status. No evidence was found to support the notion that wage deprivation was simply a manifestation of low economic position. Enduring income differences were discounted when making these evaluations. Rather, interpersonal wage comparisons were more responsive to the unfolding pattern of changes in incomes, prices, and the prospects for the economy as a whole.

RESPONSES TO DEPRIVATION

These surveys revealed that half of all working respondents felt that union strikes and nonviolent protest like picketing were sometimes the right responses to wage inequity; and one in four said not working hard or participating in a work slowdown was sometimes the right response. This support of nonmarket mechanisms to either increase wages or decrease labor inputs was balanced by more than three in four respondents stating that it was never right to do work poorly, work irregularly, or engage in protest that disrupts the public order. Overall, actions associated with reduction of individual work effort were widely viewed as unjustifiable. Collective efforts to redress wages were often viewed as appropriate, especially traditional union tactics. Collective protests that disrupt public order, however, were rarely seen as acceptable means to redress wage inequity. Similar responses, and the extent of their endorsement, were found in each of the 1973 and 1974 surveys.

In addition to wage redress tactics, this study investigated what role U.S. workers thought the federal government should play in providing for the economic welfare of its citizens. Most working respondents preferred individual responsibility to government subsidies for maintaining adequate material living standards. Nonetheless, one in four U.S. workers felt the federal government should be primarily responsible for providing adequate housing and jobs. And, for individual health care, half of all workers favored placing the primary responsibility on federal subsidy programs.

Significant differences and subgroup polarization in these views may directly contribute to a greater sense of deprivation, since social welfare is not only affected by the income distribution itself, but also by the process of distributional change. Moreover, the lack of common agreement on the means of distributional change may also weaken chances for resolution without costly disruptions. The particular tactics that are viewed as permissible to exact distributional change set limits on the consequences of such actions on production and economic stability. Analysis may well augur an increased disruptive potential, because the young and highly educated, much more often than other workers, felt that actions taken to redress wage inequity were justified, regardless of the means. On the other hand, these data may simply point to the necessary balance between the need for stability and order, and the need for change in an evolving political economy. In either case, the data provide an overview of the distributional norms in 1973-74, and can be used to gauge subsequent change.

Inequity not only justifies but also motivates income redress. Unfavorable income evaluations were shown to correspond to a more wide-ranging endorsement of tactics to gain wage redress, and to preferences for expanded federal income, housing, and health care subsidies. In moving beyond the examination of the welfare aspects of distribution, to the motivational content of sensed deprivation, these analyses investigated how relative income evaluations act to shape future income distributions. In contrast to the bases of evaluations, analysis demonstrated that it was enduring differences in relative income, rather than transitory fluctuations, that were most closely associated with these predispositions. Furthermore, while past real income progress and aspirations for future advancement did exhibit a substantial impact on current income evaluations, these factors did not demonstrate a strong or systematic direct impact on behavioral predispositions. Nevertheless, how people rated their income and standard of living did affect the predispositions, and in this manner transitory income fluctuations also indirectly affected the behavioral predispositions.

Figure 9.1 highlights how objective differences in relative socioeconomic position were differentially mediated by subjective income evaluations. In this summary display, only relationships for which the estimated associations were repeatedly documented both across types of behavioral responses and survey dates are indicated. This display excludes those relationships that were primarily related to the distinctive aspects of each particular federal subsidy program or labor market reaction, and those associations that failed to be replicated. This procedure thus draws attention to the more systematic sources of distributional change.

FIGURE 9.1

Summary Display of the Determinants of Behavioral Predispositions toward Distributional Change

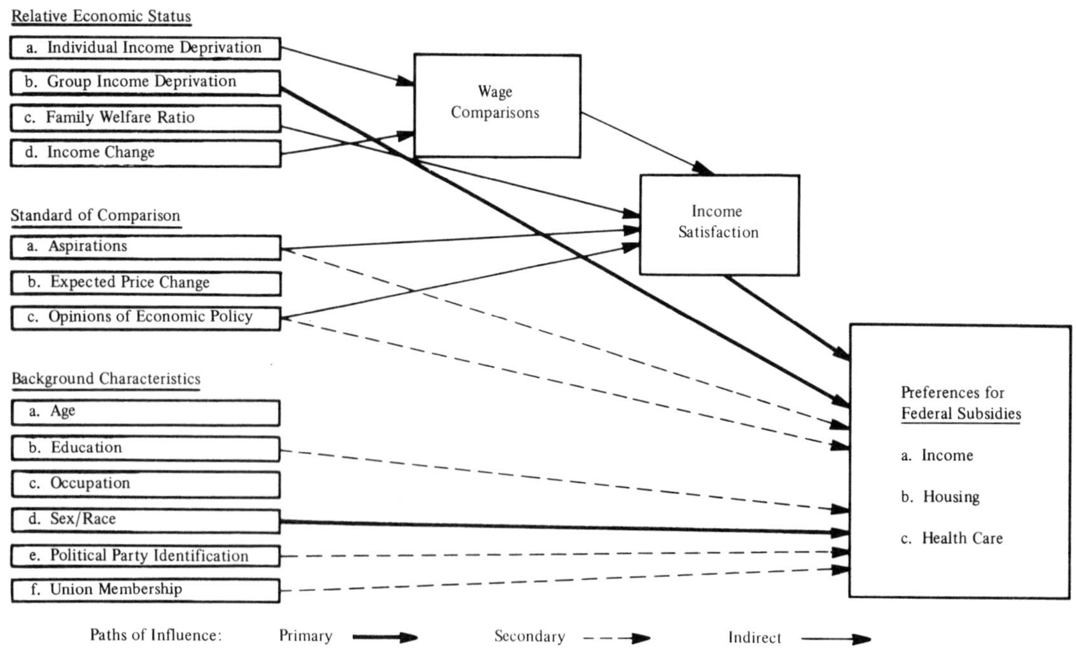

At the left of the display, the arrow connecting age, education, and occupation with individual and group income deprivation indicates their important impact on setting income reference standards. In addition to these indirect effects on reference standards, differences in age and education were directly associated with these predispositions toward change. Interestingly, however, these background characteristics did not directly affect income evaluations themselves.

As shown in the display, subjective income evaluations play a central role in the process by which actual income differences are translated into predispositions toward change. Differences in pay increases, and income differences as compared to other workers with similar skills, directly affected interpersonal wage evaluations, which in turn affected overall income satisfaction. Differences in the adequacy of income in meeting family needs, on the other hand, directly affected income satisfaction, but not wage evaluations. In each case, these transitory sources of deprivation were mediated by subjective evaluations, and only in this indirect fashion affected behavioral predispositions. These results indicate that most transitory sources of deprivation were thus insulated from directly affecting predispositions toward distributional change.

In contrast, group income deprivation, rather than being mediated by subjective evaluations, directly affected predispositions toward distributional change. Workers with few skills and little formal education more often favored expanded tactics for wage redress, and more frequently favored government subsidies. This direct association with more enduring differences in income position was maintained even apart from current wage and income evaluations.

Subjective evaluations not only depend on actual income position, but also on the standards people use for comparison. In light of the stability of subjective income evaluations over the 1973-75 period, the ready and flexible response of reference standards in the face of widespread unemployment and rapid inflation cannot be discounted. Moreover, given the central role played by subjective income evaluations, factors that prompt heightened expectations can only exacerbate calls for redress. Importantly, individual aspirations and the confidence people had in the government's ability to combat high unemployment and inflation were found to influence reported satisfaction. High individual aspirations, and lack of confidence in the government, were found to heighten dissatisfaction, and so prompt predispositions toward change.

Of particular concern for public policy, price inflation and transitory fluctuations in relative incomes were mediated by subjective income evaluations, and in turn prompted an increased readiness to utilize collective tactics or lessened productivity to gain wage redress. The resulting higher costs of production can then feed back to form the basis of renewed claims of deprivation. Transitory fluctuations in incomes, if they occur at random within the population, will not accumulate the necessary momentum for effecting distributional change. But if very many people are affected in the same way, and at the same time, waves of deprivation may develop into potent sources of economic instability. Rapidly spiraling prices provides that common experience and potent source of deprivation.

APPENDIX
SURVEY METHODS

SAMPLING AND INTERVIEWING*

The samples of the Survey Research Center represent cross sections of the population living in private households in the United States, excluding Alaska and Hawaii. Transients, residents of institutions, and persons living on military bases are not included. The method known as multistage area probability sampling is used to select a sample of dwelling units representative of the nation. The 74 sample points, located in 37 states and the District of Columbia, include the New York-northeastern New Jersey and the Chicago-northwestern Indiana consolidated areas, the ten largest standard metropolitan statistical areas (SMSAs) outside of the two standard consolidated areas, 32 other SMSAs, and 30 counties or county groups representing the nonmetropolitan and less urban portions of the country.

In the multistage area probability sample, first-stage stratification of SMSAs and counties is carried out independently within each of the four major geographical regions—the Northeast, the North Central states, the South, and West—each of which receives representation in proportion to its population. Thus, in a sample of 1,000 households, selections from the regions would be about 240, 280, 310, and 170 households, respectively.

Over all regions, the SMSAs and counties are assigned to 74 relatively homogeneous groups or strata. Twelve of these strata contain only one primary area each; these are the two Standard Consolidated Areas and the ten largest SMSAs, which are included with certainty. The remaining 62 strata average a little over two million population and may contain from two to 200 or more primary areas (SMSAs or county groups). From each stratum one primary area is selected with probability proportionate to population. This sampling process leads to approximately equal sample sizes from the 62 sample areas.

Instead of independent selections within each of the 62 strata, controlled probability selection is introduced for a more efficient sample. Within each of the four geographic regions the selections of primary areas are linked by a procedure that controls the distribution of sample areas by states and degree of urbanization beyond the controls effected through the formation of the 62

---

*Materials presented in this appendix were adapted from Richard T. Curtin, ed., *Surveys of Consumers 1974-75: Contributions to Behavioral Economics* (Ann Arbor: Institute for Social Research, University of Michigan, 1976).

strata. This controlled selection yields a more balanced sample and increases the precision of sample estimates.

As the multistage sampling continues within the 74 primary areas, the geographic area is divided and subdivided through several stages into successively smaller sampling units. By definition and procedure, each housing unit belongs uniquely to one sampling unit at each stage. There are, on the average, three to six cities, towns, and rural areas that are the secondary selections within each primary area, with somewhat more selected in the larger SMSAs. Blocks or clusters of addresses in cities and towns and chunks of rural areas are the third-stage units. In a fourth stage, depending on the size of the primary area, there is a selection of around five to ten or more small segments of about four housing units where interviews are attempted for a study. The overall sampling rate for housing units is frequently about 1/32,000. In a last stage of sampling, one respondent 18 years of age or older is selected from among eligible household members. The sample is designed to yield approximately 1,500 interviews.

Probability selection is enforced at all stages of sampling; the interviewer has no freedom of choice among housing units or among household members within a sample dwelling. Five calls, and in some cases more, are made at different times in the day at dwelling units at which no one has been found at home. If a designated respondent refuses to give relevant information, a letter is sent urging him to reconsider. The letter if followed by another visit.

The Survey Research Center maintains a nationwide staff of interviewers, selected and trained by a staff of traveling supervisors. The interviewers are instructed in the careful and uniform use of the fixed-question open-answer technique. They pay particular attention to the establishment of rapport with respondents. Many questions are answered in the respondent's own words, which the interviewers record verbatim (or as completely as possible). Nondirective probes are used to clarify the answers received.

SURVEY ERRORS

Properly conducted sample interview surveys yield useful estimates, but they do not yield exact values. Errors may arise from several sources: sampling, nonresponse, reporting, and processing. Each source of error must be considered in evaluating the accuracy of survey information. Because of these different kinds of errors, differences between current and past findings may not be significant.

Sampling errors arise in surveys because only a fraction of the population is interviewed. Since the data obtained in successive surveys are based on representative samples drawn by probability methods, the size of the sampling errors can be calculated. The magnitude of the sampling error depends on the size of the sample and its geographic spread and on the magnitude of the reported percentage in question.

The Sampling Section of the Survey Research Center has made elaborate calculations to determine the sampling errors of the major attitudinal and expectational measures used by the center.[1] Sampling errors are presented in two ways: first, as they relate to survey findings (see Table A1); second, as they relate to differences in survey findings—either differences between independent samples or differences between subgroups of the same sample (see Table A2). Sampling errors are not a measure of the actual errors involved in specific survey measurements; that is, except for nonsampling errors, errors greater than those shown in Table A1 or differences larger than those found in Table A2 will occur by chance in only five cases out of 100.

Nonresponse errors arise because some persons selected for the sample refuse to be interviewed, are not at home after repeated callbacks, are ill, or do not speak English. The response rate in the surveys reported in this book was approximately 75 percent. More than three fifths of the nonresponses resulted from refusals to be interviewed or to give important data. Much of the remainder resulted from the inability of the interviewer to contact anyone at the dwelling unit.

TABLE A1

Approximate Sampling Errors of Survey Findings (in percentages by size of sample or subgroup)

Reported	Number of Interviews						
Percentage	1,000	700	500	400	300	200	100
50	3.8	4.4	5.1	5.6	6.4	7.6	10.0
30 or 70	3.5	4.0	4.7	5.2	5.9	7.0	9.6
20 or 80	3.0	3.5	4.1	4.5	5.1	6.1	8.4
10 or 90	2.3	2.6	3.1	3.4	3.8	4.6	6.3
5 or 95	1.7	1.9	2.2	2.5	2.8	3.3	4.6

Note: The figures in this table represent two standard errors. Hence, for most items the chances are 95 in 100 that the value being estimated lies within a range equal to the reported percentages, plus or minus the sampling error.

Reporting errors—due to misunderstanding of questions or answers, lack of interest by the respondent, or intentional falsification—are kept at a minimum by careful training of interviewers, by attempting to gain the confidence and cooperation of the respondent so that he will answer to the best of his ability, and by watching for inconsistencies in the process of coding and analysis. Because answers are influenced by the wording of questions, conclusions based on answers to a single question are less reliable than those emerging from answers to

TABLE A2

Approximate Sampling Errors of Differences (in percentages)

Size of Subgroup	1,000	700	500	400	300	200	100
	For Percentages from 35 percent to 65 percent						
1,000	5.4	5.8	6.4	6.8	7.4	8.5	11.0
700		6.3	6.8	7.2	7.8	8.8	11.0
500			7.2	7.6	8.2	9.2	12.0
400				8.0	8.5	9.5	12.0
300					9.0	9.9	12.0
200						11.0	13.0
100							15.0
	For Percentages around 20 percent and 80 percent						
1,000	4.3	4.7	5.1	5.4	5.9	6.8	8.9
700		5.0	5.4	5.7	6.2	7.1	9.1
500			5.8	6.1	6.5	7.3	9.3
400				6.4	6.8	7.6	9.5
300					7.2	7.9	9.8
200						8.6	10.0
100							12.0
	For Percentages around 10 percent and 90 percent						
1,000	3.2	3.5	3.8	4.1	4.5	5.1	6.7
700		3.8	4.1	4.3	4.7	5.3	6.8
500			4.3	4.6	4.9	5.5	7.0
400				4.8	5.1	5.7	7.1
300					5.4	6.0	7.3
200						6.5	7.8
100							8.9
	For Percentages around 5 percent and 95 percent						
1,000	2.3	2.5	2.8	3.0	3.2	3.7	4.8
700		2.7	2.9	3.1	3.4	3.8	4.9
500			3.2	3.3	3.6	4.0	5.1
400				3.5	3.7	4.1	5.2
300					3.9	4.3	5.3
200						4.7	5.6
100							6.4

Note: The values shown are the percentage differences in survey findings required for significance (two standard errors).

several questions or from the interrelationship of answers to several questions. Reporting errors are minimized when comparisons are made between answers to identical questions obtained in successive surveys making use of the same methods; there is reason to assume that reporting errors have the same direction and similar magnitudes under these circumstances.

NOTE

1. See Leslie Kish, "Standard Errors for Indexes from Complex Samples," *Journal of the American Statistical Association* 63 (June 1968).

BIBLIOGRAPHY

Adams, J. Stacy. "Wage Inequities, Productivity and Work Quality." *Industrial Relations* 3 (October 1963): 9-16.

———. "Toward an Understanding of Inequity." *Journal of Abnormal and Social Psychology* 67 (November 1963): 422-36.

———. "Injustice in Social Exchange." In *Advances in Experimental Social Psychology*, vol. 2, edited by L. Berkowitz. New York: Academic Press, 1965.

Andrews, Frank M., et al. *Multiple Classification Analysis: A Report on a Computer Program for Multiple Regression Using Categorical Predictors*. 2d ed. Ann Arbor: Institute for Social Research, University of Michigan, 1973.

Arrow, Kenneth J. *Social Choice and Individual Values*. 2d ed. New York: Wiley, 1963.

Atkinson, John W. *An Introduction to Motivation*. Princeton: Van Nostrand, 1964.

Becker, Gary S. *Human Capital*. New York: National Bureau of Economic Research, 1964.

Bergson, Abram. "A Reformulation of Certain Aspects of Welfare Economics." *Quarterly Journal of Economics* 52 (February, 1938): 310-34.

Blau, Peter M. *Exchange and Power in Social Life*. New York: Wiley, 1964.

Boulding, Kenneth E. "Love, Fear and the Economist: An Interview." *Challenge* 16 (July/August, 1973): 32-39.

Breit, William, and William Culbertson. "Distributional Equality and Aggregate Utility: Comment." *American Economic Review* 60 (June 1970): 435-41.

Brennan, Geoffrey. "Pareto Desirable Redistribution: The Case of Malice and Envy," *Journal of Public Economics* 2 (April 1973): 173-83.

Brickman, Phillip, and Donald T. Campbell. "Hedonic Relativism and Planning the Good Society." In *Adaptation Level Theory: A Symposium*, edited by M. H. Appley. New York: Academic Press, 1972.

Buchanan, James M., and William C. Stubblebine. "Externality." *Economica* 29 (November 1962): 371-84.

Buchanan, James M., and Gordon Tullock. *The Calculus of Consent*. Ann Arbor: University of Michigan Press, 1965.

Campbell, Donald T., and Julian C. Stanley. *Experimental and Quasi-Experimental Designs for Research*. Chicago: Rand McNally, 1966.

Curtin, Richard T., Buckhard Strumpel, and Gerald Gurin. *Economic Incentives, Values, and Subjective Well-Being*. Ann Arbor: Social Science Archive, Institute for Social Research, University of Michigan, 1976.

Curtin, Richard T., and Charles D. Cowan. "Public Attitudes Toward Fiscal Programs." In *Surveys of Consumers 1972-73: Contributions to Behavioral Economics*, edited by Burkhard Strumpel et al. Ann Arbor: Institute for Social Research, University of Michigan, 1975.

Curtin, Richard T., ed. *Surveys of Consumers 1974-75: Contributions to Behavioral Economics*. Ann Arbor: Institute for Social Research, University of Michigan, 1976.

Curtin, Richard T. "Well-Being, Goals, and Motivations for Economic Advancement." In *Economic Means for Human Needs*, edited by Burkhard Strumpel. Ann Arbor: Institute for Social Research, University of Michigan, 1976.

Davis, James A. "A Formal Interpretation of the Theory of Relative Deprivation." *Sociometry* 22 (December 1959): 280-96.

Duncan, Greg J., and Charles D. Cowan. "Labor Market Discrimination and Nonpecuniary Work Rewards." In *Surveys of Consumers 1972-73: Contributions to Behavioral Economics*, edited by Burkhard Strumpel et al. Ann Arbor: Institute for Social Research, University of Michigan, 1975.

Duesenberry, James S. *Income, Savings, and the Theory of Consumer Behavior*. Cambridge: Harvard University Press, 1949.

Festinger, Leon A. *A Theory of Cognitive Dissonance*. Stanford: Stanford University Press, 1957.

——. "A Theory of Social Comparison Processes." *Human Relations* 7 (June 1954): 117-40.

Friedman, Milton. *A Theory of the Consumption Function*. Princeton: Princeton University Press, 1957.

Glintis, Herbert. "A Radical Analysis of Welfare Economics and Individual Development." *Quarterly Journal of Economics* 86 (November 1972): 572-99.

Goodman, Paul S. "An Examination of Referents Used in the Evaluation of Pay." *Organizational Behavior and Human Performance* 12 (October 1974): 170-95.

Graaff, Johannes de V. *Theoretical Welfare Economics*. Cambridge, England: Cambridge University Press, 1957.

Gurin, Gerald, and Patricia Gurin. "Expectancy Theory in the Study of Poverty." *Journal of Social Issues* 26 (Spring 1970): 83-104.

Gurr, Ted R. *Why Men Rebel*. Princeton: Princeton University Press, 1970.

Harmon, H. H. *Modern Factor Analysis*. 2d ed. Chicago: University of Chicago Press, 1967.

Harsanyi, John. "Cardinal Utility in Welfare Economics and the Theory of Risk Taking." *Journal of Political Economy* 61 (October 1953): 434-35.

Hirschman, Albert O. "The Changing Tolerance for Income Inequality." *Quarterly Journal of Economics* 87 (November 1973): 544-66.

Hochman, Harold M. "Individual Preferences and Distributional Adjustments." *American Economic Review* 62 (May 1972): 353-60.

Hochman, Harold M., and George E. Peterson, eds. *Redistribution Through Public Choice.* New York: Columbia University Press, 1974.

Hochman, Harold M., and James D. Rodgers. "Pareto Optimal Redistribution." *American Economic Review* 59 (September 1969): 542-57.

Homans, George C. *Social Behavior: Its Elementary Forms.* New York: Harcourt, Brace, and World, 1961.

Hyman, Herbert H. "The Psychology of Status." *Archives of Psychology* 38 (1942): 15.

Jacques, Elliott. *Equitable Payment.* New York: Wiley, 1961.

Juster, F. Thomas, ed. *Education, Income, and Human Behavior.* New York: McGraw-Hill, 1975.

Kaldor, Nicholas. "Welfare Propositions and Interpersonal Comparisons of Utility." *Economic Journal* 49 (September 1939): 549-52.

Katona, George. *Psychological Economics.* New York: Elsevier, 1975.

Katona, George, Burkhard Strumpel, and Ernest Zahn. *Aspirations and Affluence: Comparative Studies in the United States and Western Europe.* New York: McGraw-Hill, 1971.

Kish, Leslie. "Standard Errors for Indexes from Complex Samples." *Journal of the American Statistical Association* 63 (June 1968).

Lancaster, Kelvin J. "A New Approach to Consumer Theory." *Journal of Political Economy* 74 (April 1966): 132-57.

Lawler, Edward E. *Pay and Organizational Effectiveness.* New York: McGraw-Hill, 1971.

——. "Equity Theory as a Predictor of Productivity and Work Quality." *Psychological Bulletin* 70 (December 1968): 596-610.

Little, I. M. D. *A Critique of Welfare Economics.* 2d ed. Oxford, England: Oxford University Press, 1957.

Lydall, Harold. *The Structure of Earnings.* Oxford, England: Clarendon Press, 1968.

Mill, John Stuart. *Principles of Political Economy*, edited by J. M. Robson. Toronto: University of Toronto Press, 1965.

Mincer, Jacob. *Schooling, Experience, and Earnings.* New York: National Bureau of Economic Research, 1974.

——. "The Distribution of Labor Incomes: A Survey with Special Reference to the Human Capital Approach." *Journal of Economic Literature* 8 (March 1970): 1-27.

——. "Education Experience and the Distribution of Earnings and Employment." in *Education, Income, and Human Behavior*, edited by F. Thomas Juster. New York: National Bureau of Economic Research, 1975.

Mishan, Ezra J. *Welfare Economics: An Assessment.* Amsterdam: North-Holland, 1969.

——. "A Survey of Welfare Economics, 1939-1959." *Economic Journal* 70 (June 1960): 197-265.

Modigliani, Franco, and Brumberg, Richard. "Utility Analysis and the Consumption Function: An Interpretation of Cross-Section Data." In *Post-Keynesian Economics*, edited by Kenneth Kurihara. New Brunswick: Rutgers University Press, 1954.

Musgrave, Richard A. *The Theory of Public Finance.* New York: McGraw-Hill, 1959.

Okun, Arthur M. *Equality and Efficiency: The Big Tradeoff*, Washington, D.C.: The Brookings Institution, 1975.

Pauly, Mark V. "Optimality, Public Goods, and Local Governments: A General Theoretical Analysis." *Journal of Political Economy* 78 (May/June 1970): 572-85.

Pauly, Mark V. and Thomas D. Willett. "Two Concepts of Equity and their Implications for Public Policy." *Social Science Quarterly* 53 (June 1972): 8-19.

Pettigrew, Thomas F. "Social Evaluation Theory: Contingencies and Applications." In *Nebraska Symposium on Motivation: 1967*, edited by David Levine. Lincoln: University of Nebraska Press, 1967.

Petty, Sir William. *The Economic Writings of Sir William Petty*, edited by C. H. Hall. Cambridge, England: Cambridge University Press, 1899.

Phelps, Edmund S., ed. *Economic Justice: Selected Readings.* Baltimore: Penguin, 1973.

Pigou, A. C. *The Economics of Welfare.* 4th ed. London: Macmillan, 1960.

Rainwater, Lee. *What Money Buys: Inequality and the Social Meanings of Income.* New York: Basic Books, 1974.

Rawls, John. *A Theory of Justice.* Cambridge: Harvard University Press, 1971.

Robbins, Lionel. *An Essay on the Nature and Significance of Economic Science.* London: Macmillan, 1937.

Robinson, Joan. "The Second Crisis of Economic Theory." *American Economic Review* 62 (May 1972): 1-10.

Rogers, James D. "Explaining Income Redistribution." In *Redistribution Through Public Choice*, edited by Harold M. Hochman and George E. Peterson. New York: Columbia University Press, 1974.

Rothenberg, Jerome. *The Measurement of Social Welfare*. New York: Prentice-Hall, 1961.

Rozeboom, W. W. *Foundations of the Theory of Prediction*. Homewood, Ill.: Dorsey Press, 1966.

Runciman, Walter G. *Relative Deprivation and Social Justice*. Berkeley: University of California Press, 1966.

Samuelson, Paul A. *Foundations of Economic Analysis*. Cambridge: Harvard University Press, 1947.

Schmolders, Gunter, and Bernd Biervert, "Level of Aspiration and Consumption Standard: Some General Findings." In *Human Behavior in Economic Affairs*, edited by Burkhard Strumpel, James N. Morgan, and Ernest Zahn, pp. 213-27. New York: Elsevier Scientific Publishing Co., 1972.

Scitovsky, Tibor. "A Note on Welfare Propositions in Economics." *Review of Economic Studies* 9 (November 1941): 77-88.

Slutsky, Eugen E. "On the Theory of the Budget of the Consumer." In *Readings in Price Theory*, edited by George J. Stigler and Kenneth E. Boulding. Chicago: Irwin, 1952.

Stouffer, S. A., et al. *The American Soldier: Adjustments During Army Life*. Princeton: Princeton University Press, 1949.

Strumpel, Burkhard, ed. *Economic Means for Human Needs*. Ann Arbor: Institute for Social Research, University of Michigan, 1976.

Strumpel, Burkhard, James N. Morgan, and Ernest Zahn, eds. *Human Behavior in Economic Affairs: Essays in Honor of George Katona*. Amsterdam: Elsevier Scientific Publishing Co., 1972.

Thibaut, John W., and Harold H. Kelley. *The Social Psychology of Groups*. New York: Wiley, 1959.

Thurow, Lester C. "The Income Distribution as a Pure Public Good." *Quarterly Journal of Economics* 85 (May 1971): 327-36.

——. "Toward a Definition of Economic Justice." *Public Interest* 31 (Spring 1973): 50-65.

Vanneman, Reeve D., and Thomas F. Pettigrew. "Race and Relative Deprivation in the Urban United States." *Race* 13 (April 1972): 461-86.

Von Furstenberg, George M., and Dennis C. Mueller. "The Pareto Optimal Approach to Redistribution: A Fiscal Application." *American Economic Review* 61 (September 1971): 628-37.

ABOUT THE AUTHOR

RICHARD T. CURTIN is Director of the Surveys of Consumer Attitudes at the Survey Research Center, and Assistant Professor of Economics, at The University of Michigan.

Dr. Curtin has published several articles reporting on his research in behavioral economics, including perceptions of economic well-being, reactions to changing economic opportunities, and public policy preferences. His reports on current trends in consumer attitudes and expectations appear quarterly in *Economic Outlook: USA*, and other publications. He is the editor of the volume *Surveys of Consumers 1974-75: Contributions to Behavioral Economics*.

Dr. Curtin holds a B.A. from Michigan State University, and a Ph.D. in Economics from the University of Michigan. This book represents an outgrowth of his dissertation *Perceptions of Distributional Equity: Their Economic Bases and Consequences*. Recently, he has served as a consultant to the Committee on Measurement of Energy Consumption, National Academy of Sciences, and has presented papers at the Annual Meetings of the Economic, Psychological, and Statistical Associations.

RELATED TITLES
Published by
Praeger Special Studies

EMPLOYMENT, INCOME, AND WELFARE IN THE RURAL SOUTH
Brian Rungeling
Lewis H. Smith
Vernan M. Briggs, Jr.
John F. Adams

EQUITY, INCOME, AND POLICY: Comparative Studies in Three Worlds of Development
edited by
Irving Louis Horowitz

*A FULL EMPLOYMENT PROGRAM FOR THE 1970s
edited by
Alan Gartner
William Lynch, Jr.
Frank Riessman

THE LABOR SUPPLY FOR LOWER-LEVEL OCCUPATIONS
Harold Wool

OCCUPATIONAL CHOICES AND TRAINING NEEDS: Prospects for the 1980s
Leonard A. Lecht

QUALITY OF LIFE INDICATORS IN U.S. METROPOLITAN AREAS: A Statistical Analysis
Ben-Chieh Liu

*Also available in paperback as a PSS Student Edition